THE BIG CARROT
VEGETARIAN
COOKBOOK

THE BIG CARROT

VEGETARIAN

COOKBOOK

RECIPES FROM THE KITCHEN OF THE BIG CARROT

by

Anne Lukin

SECOND STORY *Press*

CANADIAN CATALOGUING IN PUBLICATION DATA

Main entry under title:
The Big Carrot vegetarian cookbook
ISBN 0-929005-05-8
1. Vegetarian cookery.   2. Menus.   I. Lukin, Anne.
II. Big Carrot Natural Food Market.

TX837.B53 1989   641.5'636   C89-095306-6

Printed and Bound in Canada

Published by
SECOND STORY PRESS
585 ½ Bloor St. West
Toronto M6G 1K5

CONTENTS

ACKNOWLEDGEMENTS

As I have worked developing, testing, editing and compiling the recipes and information in this book, I have relied on many people for ideas and help. Much of the credit for this book goes to:

❧ The wonderful cooks of The Big Carrot kitchen, who developed and cooked these recipes over the years. This book is a direct result of their talent, creativity and love of food.

Gladys Amaya, Sarah Ayerst, Aziza Bellair, Sharon E. Bishop, Martin Cerrone, David Cohlmeyer, Buck Cywink, John Ghitan, Meri Hanlin, Kar-in Hansen, Debra Hayes, Nelly Hotke, Yo James, Akemi Kobayashi, Brad LaMarsh, Anne Lukin, Herbert Pryke, Luanne Rayvals, Paula Ring, Susan Towers, Rita Yeatts

❧ John Ghitan for co-writing the Introduction, his many contributions, his flair in the kitchen and his wonderful Romanian mother.

❧ All our co-workers at The Big Carrot, who keep the kitchen supplied with carrots and camaraderie.

❧ The many people who tested these recipes for home use.

❧ The women of Second Story Press for their expertise, encouragement and willingness to back this project.

❧ The copy editor, Pamela Cross, for her careful attention to detail, and her experienced, helpful advice.

❧ The illustrator, Sally Davies, whose beautiful drawings grace the book.

❧ Douglas Harris, who generously loaned his computer for the writing of this book; Aziza Bellair for typing and contributions to the Glossary; and Heather S. Dell for her editorial suggestions.

❧ Mary Lou Morgan, for her support and contributions during the writing of this book. Without her conviction, it wouldn't have happened.

❧ The farmers and suppliers who are working to produce healthy food, and who make it possible for us to offer a growing selection of chemical-free foods.

❧ Our customers, who keep coming back and asking for more.

Thanks!

ON A PERSONAL NOTE

A grateful dedication of my efforts on this book to my grandmothers, Gertrude Levine Lukin and Eileen Segrist Leeth, who taught me about the blessings of a full heart and a full plate. A bushel and a peck and a hug around the neck.

Thanks to my friends and parents who have given me support through the sometimes crazy task of putting this book together; for your laughter and interest and helpful suggestions and for all the distractions along the way. A special thanks to my kitchenmates for putting up with all the hoo-ha. With heartfelt thanks to so many others (you know who you are).

Anne Lukin
May 1989

❧ INTRODUCTION ❧

"Why another cookbook?" you ask as you browse through this one. "And who, or what, is THE BIG CARROT?!?" you might also wonder. Well, The Big Carrot, in Toronto, is one of Canada's largest natural food markets, with our own vegetarian kitchen and deli. And because so many of our customers have asked for recipes from our kitchen over the years, we're finally obliging them with some of their favourites. We believe we have a thoughtful but non-dogmatic approach to a world of delicious, healthy food, that we'd like to share beyond the reach of our deli counter. Using high quality ingredients, fresh produce and whole grains, we have tapped the world's great ethnic cuisines to create dishes that incorporate alternative dietary concepts to meet specific needs, while still appealing to people who just love good food.

More and more people are becoming interested in nutrition and the effects of diet on health. As well, there has been a phenomenal growth in the amount of information available about food, whether on a personal or global scale — from allergies to the long-term impact of the use of chemicals in food production. In this context, we offer an introduction to new foods and new ideas. The recipes in this book are like a sampler of the multitude of thoughts and concerns addressing the way we humans should eat.

Should is a terrible word, especially to a cook. Especially to a cook who grew up on fried chicken smothered in cream gravy served with mounds of mashed potatoes (and gravy) and hot biscuits (with butter and gravy) and ice cream for dessert. Or to another cook who was weaned on cognac-rich patés, seafood vol-au-vents, stroganoff finished with Devon cream, homemade buttered egg noodles and eight-layer chocolate buttercream cakes. In fact, all the cooks who have worked in our kitchen have brought with them their own rich heritage of cooking styles. The motivation behind the foods we grew up on was quite simply good taste, with a hazy nod in the general direction of the "four food groups." But increasingly, we are giving serious thought to how we can ensure that food that tastes good is good for us as well. We are, more and more, shaping our cooking to reflect the information we are receiving about nutrition, allergies and general health. Certainly the cooks at The Big Carrot have been faced with these ideas, and have created dishes that respond to one or more of these theories, with great success.

There are many reasons why people may want or need to change their diet to include more whole grains and more fresh produce. There are many stages of evolution along the road to a healthy diet, and there is no one diet which fits every individual's needs. If you are already eating "whole foods," these recipes may give you ideas for new combinations and new spicings so that you can further enjoy a healthy diet. If you are just beginning to experiment with moving away from a mainstream Western diet, you may want to ease into new ingredients slowly, gradually building up a new repertoire of dishes and accustoming yourself to new tastes. Remember that it took a long time to learn to eat as you do now, that favourite tastes were acquired over years, and that you should not expect to unlearn a lifetime of eating habits overnight. Whole grains and fresh vegetables *do* taste differently (deliciously different, we believe) from packaged, processed, refined ingredients, and you may need to acquire a taste for them the same way you acquired a taste for peanut butter or ice cream as a child.

Just as our recipes have evolved over the years as we have incorporated new ideas about food, so The Big Carrot itself has grown up out of changing consumer habits. The store sprang from the convictions of a group of people that the foods that we choose to eat carry implications that spread out beyond our own lives. It has grown in much the same way that the organic movement itself has grown, with struggle and perseverance and trial and error.

On a hot Saturday morning in 1983, nine people pounded the pavement in Toronto's east side, clipboards in hand, asking people provocative questions like, "Is organic produce important to you?" and "How much do you spend on health food in a month?" The nine had previously worked together in a health food store, where working conditions had left them burned out, underfinanced, and finally, unemployed. Despite this, or perhaps because of it, they were still fired with enthusiasm for setting up their own natural food store. They wanted to offer customers a full and varied selection of quality natural foods (organic whenever possible), with friendly, informed service, while securing employment and self-management for themselves through a worker co-op structure. They faced the obstacles of high rents, skeptical bank managers, and competition, with "Gumption," some would say. "Bloody crazy leftover '60s idealism," others might mutter under their breath.

Nevertheless, from these humble beginnings, like a large orange and green phoenix, rose "The Big Carrot." Nine original founders scrambled for capital, mortgaged their homes, cosigned their parents and firstborns, drew up business plans and opened the doors on November 18, 1983. They shared the tasks of cashiering, washing lettuce, of long-range planning and bagging groceries. They were obviously in the right place at the right time with a bright idea, because business grew and grew. After only three years in business, The Big Carrot's popularity had outgrown its floor space. Through the generosity of a local developer and cooperation with a family who owned the property across the street from the store, The Big Carrot was able to move in October, 1987, to a new store three times the size of its original location. They also helped develop the surrounding shopping mall of "alternative" retailers and professionals.

Today, The Big Carrot offers products ranging from dried seaweed to fresh organic produce and meat, as well as prepared foods from its own kitchens. It specializes in hard-to-get items for vegetarians, macrobiotic diets, people suffering from acute allergies, people on special diets and people who are just interested in good health and good food. The common factor behind the foods and products sold at the The Big Carrot is that they are all in as natural a state as possible, free from additives, preservatives, pesticides and other questionable chemical compounds. Whenever possible, certified organic products are made available. And people are eating it up.

There's a lot of hard work and good will that has gone into the making of this success story. But perhaps the biggest determining factor of this store's popularity has been that the market for "clean food" is definitely a large and growing one. There seems to be no question that people are becoming increasingly aware of what they are eating. And aware of the crisis situations that are brewing in our world because of overuse of chemicals, misuse of the world's resources and food supply, and abuse of the environment. Our customers want to do what they can to maintain control over what they eat, and contribute to a cleaner, more sane and sustainable system of agriculture by using a powerful grass-roots tool; spending their dollars and consuming in a way that supports the spread of healthier food. The Big Carrot is doing whatever it can to foster these ends by actively encouraging local organic farmers and producers and by educating the public about these issues.

These very concerns may explain why you are reading this cookbook in the first place, suspiciously eyeing your coffee and muffin at the same time. Our personal health is certainly as directly dependent on our diet as it is on genetics, luck and bad habits. The continued health and survival of our world is dependent on cleaning up our act, both literally and figuratively. New information, theories and food products are appearing almost daily; concerned people are exploring and experimenting. And naturally, out of all this, new demands are being made of "those who cook." That's where this book comes in...

The recipes in this book utilize a wide variety of alternative ingredients, as replacements for more traditional ingredients, or simply for their own merits. Soybean products (tofu, tempeh, soymilk), nonwheat flours, nonsugar sweeteners (honey, maple syrup, rice malt), sea vegetables and other "macrobiotic" products: all these and more are important parts of our recipes. None of these ingredients is particularly new, but for those not familiar with them, our recipes offer an accessible approach to these products. We feel that these recipes should act as a springboard for new ideas, new foods, new favourites.

What we hope is that this cookbook represents the *possibilities*, not the limitations, of changing how and what we eat for increased health, without forfeiting good taste. It is the customers of The Big Carrot themselves who are the proof of the dairy-free pudding (so to speak). Their continued patronage, interest and requests have resulted in this book. It is our response to our customers' ultimate compliment, "This tastes great! Will you marry me, or at least give me the recipe?"

KITCHEN ADVICE

INGREDIENTS

"Starting from scratch" with fresh, unadulterated ingredients is getting back to the basics of cooking; producing food that is less processed and better for you. While not as easy or as fast as opening a can, there is something intrinsically satisfying about preparing a meal from whole ingredients, something inherently beautiful in a mountain of fresh vegetables thoughtfully sliced, turning a cutting board into a palette of colour and texture.

We cook from fresh ingredients as much as possible, using canned ingredients only in the case of the more exotic items (baby corn, water chestnuts, etc.) and some basics such as frozen corn and peas. And even then we hunt for brands packaged without chemical additives. We also use bottled spring water in our soups, and recommend the use of it in cooking. We try to use foods that are less processed and thus retain more food value; using brown rice instead of the white rice more common in this country; cider vinegar in place of white distilled vinegar; and maple syrup or rice syrup rather than white granulated sugar.

We use organic vegetables whenever possible. They are often not as "perfect" in appearance as the chemically-enhanced, mass-produced food we have grown used to in the stores, but often that appearance of perfection is a deceptive front. Organic produce makes up in flavour what it sometimes lacks in cosmetic vanity, and each bite tastes even better with the knowledge that the fruit or vegetable was not sprayed with petro-chemicals harmful to humans and the environment.

PERSONAL PREFERENCE

Food is a very personal matter, so we expect you to alter these recipes to suit your individual taste, substituting or omitting ingredients to fit your own and your family's preferences and dietary practices. Omit the salt, heap on the chilis, substitute barley flour for wheat, do whatever you need to do to make these dishes your own favourites, with our blessings. If you are reducing salt in your diet, you may find that increasing the amount of other spices used helps keep the food from tasting bland.

EQUIPMENT

We cannot urge strongly enough the wonder and usefulness of good quality knives that are kept sharp through careful handling and the use of stone and steel. You are less likely to get cut using a sharp knife as it won't slip off vegetables the way a dull one can. Always wash and dry your knives separately, immediately after using them, and store in a knife block or rack. Don't let them bang around in a cutlery drawer, as this dulls them and is unsafe as well. Learn and practice the habit of cutting vegetables into attractive shapes appropriate to each dish instead of hurriedly whacking them all into chunks every time. Once mastered, this habit will be just as fast and will produce dishes that are as pleasing to the eye as they are to the palate. Once you get the hang of using a sharp knife, you will find you are cutting much faster, serving prettier dishes and generally feeling like Julia Child. You will never go back to dull, bent knives that you inherited when you moved away from home. Trust us.

A word about woks — those versatile bowl-shaped pans from the Orient that have become well-known in this country in the last few years. A skillet or sauté pan can be substituted if you don't have a wok, but we highly recommend purchasing one as its usefulness is not limited to Oriental dishes. When you are through with the wok, rinse it immediately with hot water, wipe it clean and dry and then wipe it very lightly with oil. Do NOT wash in soap and water, and do not leave soaking in water.

We use stainless steel pots and bowls because they are sturdy, rustproof and do not transfer tastes to or from food. This is also in response to some concerns being raised about possible side effects from cooking with aluminum cookware. We also have some concerns about the prolonged use of microwaves, so we use conventional gas ovens at The Big Carrot, and have not provided instructions for microwave cooking with these recipes.

We do use a food processor for many of our dishes; if a recipe can be duplicated by hand using a knife or whisk, we have indicated so in the recipe.

MEASUREMENTS AND CONVERSIONS

We have used cups, tablespoons, pounds and Fahrenheit in this cookbook, in the belief that these measures are still the most commonly used in cooking in both Canada and the United States and that to list both cups and millilitres for each ingredient would be cumbersome and potentially confusing. Below you will find helpful information on general measurement equivalents and converting back and forth to metric.

IMPERIAL MEASUREMENTS

3 teaspoons = 1 tablespoon
16 tablespoons = 1 cup

Volume (Liquid Measure): 8 ounces = 1 cup = ½ pint
16 ounces = 2 cups = 1 pint
32 ounces = 4 cups = 1 quart
64 ounces = 8 cups = ½ gallon
128 ounces = 16 cups = 1 gallon

Weight (Dry Measure): 16 ounces = 1 pound

CONVERSION TO METRIC

Imperial: 1 teaspoon = 5 millilitres
3 teaspoons = 1 tablespoon = 15 millilitres
1 cup = approximately 250 millilitres = ¼ litre
1 inch = approximately 2.5 centimetres

Volume: 1 cup = approximately 250 millilitres
4 cups = approximately 1000 millilitres = 1 litre

Weight: 1 ounce = approximately 30 grams
1 pound = approximately 450 grams
2.2 pounds = 1 kilogram

ABBREVIATIONS

tsp. = teaspoon
Tbsp. = tablespoon
" = inch
oz. = ounce
lb. = pound
ml = millilitre
F = Fahrenheit

COOKING TERMS FROM A TO Z

If you already know your way around a kitchen, this section will not be of paramount importance to you, although you might find it helpful to glance over the following terms and make sure that when we say sauté we mean the same sauté that you mean. There will, however, be some people who want to use this cookbook who do not know the difference between a sauté and a soufflé, and who wouldn't know a julienne if it jumped up and bit them. These people should not be the least bit ashamed of their ignorance, but perhaps should trade in a bit of their bliss for some practical cooking help by reading the following section. You will find guidelines for kitchen rituals such as zesting, mincing, dicing, slicing and making thousands of julienne fries, without the help of a Ronco gadget.

In order to save space and avoid repetition on the recipe pages, we have included more precise instructions and details here, so if you run into confusion about when you should be sautéeing and when stir frying, turn to this section for help. Please note that these are not necessarily dictionary definitions, but rather the processes that we suggest you use when we call for a particular technique in a recipe. We trust that you will adapt the techniques, measurements, spicings and almost everything else about these recipes to suit your own tastes, once you are comfortable and familiar with them.

Al dente — an Italian phrase meaning "to the tooth." Pasta that is "al dente" has been cooked until it is firm — neither raw in the middle nor mushy. Different kinds and shapes of noodles require different cooking times, so you'll have to use your own judgment, and your own "dentes." Fresh pasta can be counted on to cook in about a third of the time that dried pasta requires. See *Shocking* entry for cooking technique.

Blanching — a method of very briefly boiling vegetables. Place at least two times the amount of water for the vegetables you have in a pot large enough to hold both water and vegetables with room left over. Bring the water to a rolling boil. Leave the heat on high, add washed and sliced vegetables for 60 to 120 seconds (we're not kidding, don't get distracted and roam off). Strain or drain them from the boiling water, then place immediately in a bowl of very cold water to cover. This will stop the cooking process, and keep the vegetables from turning to mush. Blanching is meant to brighten the colour of vegetables while leaving them fairly crisp and not really cooked — not too far from raw, but more welcoming to the tooth. It is also the method used for peeling tomatoes and some fruits (peaches, etc.) easily.

Boil — to heat water or other liquid in a pot over medium-high to high heat until it bubbles. A **rapid or rolling boil** means that the entire surface is constantly agitated by large bubbles that rise from the bottom.

Chiffonade — a technique of stacking flat lettuce, spinach and other leafy greens, rolling them in a cylindrical shape like a cigar and then cutting them in very thin cross sections to form thin ribbons or shreds.

Chop — to cut into pieces or cubes with a knife. Chopping usually refers to larger pieces than dicing.

Crescents — to cut vegetables, especially onions, into thin, curving strips.

Deep-fat Frying — It's scary, a little dangerous and not very good for you, so we rarely do it. You won't be asked to fry anything in this book. If you occasionally have to indulge your weakness for a crusty fried thing, do what we do; go out and buy it.

Dice — to cut up vegetables in even, consistent pieces the size of the tip of your index finger. (Although that is where any connection between dicing and the ends of your fingers should come to a screeching halt.)

Finely dice — to cut up vegetables in even, consistent pieces the size of a kernel of corn.

Emulsify — to mix oils and other liquids together in such a way that they form a stable, thicker blend that does not separate back into its component parts. To emulsify a salad dressing, mix together the seasonings with water, lemon juice or vinegar as desired. Then while whisking vigorously or blending in food processor, slowly trickle in the oil in a steady stream.

Grate — to reduce whole pieces of food, such as cheese or carrots, into small particles, using a handheld grater or the grater wheel of a food processor (finely grated, or smaller particles, are usually referred to as shredded).

Julienne — to cut vegetables in even, consistent long thin pieces the size and shape of wooden matches, or slightly larger.

Knead — to work dough or pastry by hand until it is thoroughly mixed, elastic and smooth. Fold dough over on itself and push edges to the centre with the heel of the hand while turning the dough in a circle. How the dough is kneaded will affect the consistency and texture of the finished product (but be careful here, more is NOT always better when it comes to kneading pastry).

Mince — to cut (fresh herbs or garlic, e.g.) with a good sharp knife so finely that the pieces are about the size of the head of a pin. Garlic can alternately be pressed through a garlic press, minced with a knife, or processed in a food processor.

Sauté — To cook prepared vegetables or other food in an open skillet or pan over medium high heat in a small amount of oil, butter or margarine, while stirring often, usually for only a few minutes at a time. It is necessary to add the oil to the skillet first and bring it to medium high heat before adding the food. You are not trying to fry or sear or brown something to bits; just cook the food until it is somewhat tender. It should still have some life and a bit of crunch to it, unless we tell you otherwise.

Scorch — the disaster that occurs when the contents of a pot begin to burn along the bottom, leaving a brown sticky residue on the pot and giving the food a characteristic unpleasant smell and taste of burned food. Avoid this by using heavy-bottomed pots, paying careful attention while cooking, reducing heat as needed and stirring often. Don't get so distracted that you leave a pot on high heat unintentionally. If disaster strikes, you can try to rescue the food by immediately switching the contents to a clean pot and cooking over lower heat. Sometimes adding a dash of sweetener or a tart taste such as lemon juice or vinegar can help mask the burned taste if it is not too bad.

Shocking — a technique of cooking pasta that allows it to cook thoroughly in the middle without becoming mushy on the outside. Bring water to a rapid boil in a large pot. Add the pasta, and as soon as the water begins to boil again, add a small amount of cold water, just enough to stop the boiling. Repeat this process every time the water returns to a boil, until the pasta is cooked through to the centre. It takes a little longer, but assures that the outer layer of pasta does not cook faster than the inside. Especially useful for dense or intricately shaped pastas such as rotini, though we use it for all kinds.

Shred — to cut into very thin strips, or shreds, as in cabbage for coleslaw. Alternately, to finely grate food, such as cheese, into very small pieces.

Simmer — to cook in a pot over low to medium heat, just below the boiling point, so that tiny bubbles form along edges of pan, but the food does not actively boil.

Steam — a method of preparing food by suspending it over, not in, boiling water. The food is cooked by the heat of the steam rising through it. Use a wide-mouthed pot with a lid, and an Oriental bamboo steamer or a metal steamer or colander. The pot should contain one half-inch to one inch of water in the bottom, which should be checked during the cooking — more may need to be added to keep the pot from boiling dry. Leftover cooking water can be used in soups or sauces. Steaming vegetables is preferable to boiling them, as fewer nutrients are lost during steaming.

Stir fry — an Oriental method of cooking food very quickly with a small amount of hot oil in a wok or skillet, stirring almost constantly. The oil must be hot when you add the food, which is added in order, with food requiring longer cooking time going in first, followed by items which take less cooking. The whole procedure will take no more than 4 to 5 minutes over high heat. This leaves the vegetables flavourful and crisp.

Toss — to mix ingredients by tumbling lightly together in a bowl, using a lifting motion with fork or hands.

Zest — the word for both the process and the end product — grated rind of citrus fruit (oranges, lemons and limes, usually), used to add flavour and flecks of colour. As much as possible, use unblemished fruit that has not been sprayed with chemicals, rinse it well and grate only the topmost layer of coloured rind, using the fine grate on a handheld grater or a special tool called a zester which peels off small strips of rind. Try not to take too much of the white under the coloured rind, and try not to take too much of the skin off your knuckles; neither is desirable.

SOUPS

Ah, soup... the very word conjures images of comfort, safety and good eating. Whether with eloquence or humble sincerity, soup speaks volumes. It can play many roles, from the opening scene of a well-orchestrated dinner party, to the hero of a cold winter's day.

At the store, we lovingly prepare a big pot of soup daily, its character based on what's in season. Or sometimes we set the scene with stove-top travelogues, using the stock pot to reflect whatever exotic clime the cook is longing to be in that day. Soups allow us to exercise our creative muscles. We often concoct a daily story to explain the soup, which sometimes proves to be as much of a creative challenge as the soup itself. We have fun with the stories, as with the soups. Included are a few for you to sample.

MISO VEGETABLE (HAPPY BUDDHA) SOUP

*A weekly favourite, quick to prepare. As delicious
as it is healthy and soothing, it can help purify
the blood and ward off colds.*

SERVES 4

6 dried shiitake mushrooms
1 cup spring water

In a separate small pot, boil shiitakes in water for 5 minutes. Remove from heat and let soak for 20 minutes. Drain and reserve liquid, remove and discard stems, slice shiitakes thinly and add to soup.

5 cups spring water
¼ cup tamari

Bring water to a boil in a 4-quart pot. Add tamari and shiitake liquid.

½ cup green onions, sliced on thin diagonal
½ cup peeled & grated fresh daikon radish
½ cup peeled & julienned carrot
½ cup shredded Napa cabbage
1 cup thinly sliced mushrooms

Add vegetables to boiling water, reduce heat and simmer gently for 5 minutes. Reduce heat to low.

¼ cup toasted sesame oil
½ cup burdock root, scrubbed & sliced on thin diagonal
3 cloves garlic, minced
2 inch piece fresh ginger, peeled & grated

Heat oil in a wok until hot. Stir fry burdock, garlic and ginger for 5 minutes over medium-high heat. Spoon contents of wok into soup pot, making sure that soup is below the boiling point.

CONTINUED

¼ cup brown rice miso
1 Tbsp. umeboshi plum paste
(optional)
1 cup bean sprouts

Remove 2 cups hot broth from the pot. Add miso and umeboshi to this, stirring to dissolve, then return to soup pot. Add tamari and bean sprouts. Taste and adjust seasonings. Serve hot but do not allow to boil.

HAPPY BUDDHA SOUP

BUDDHA IS ALMOST ALWAYS PICTURED WITH A SERENE AND TENDER SMILE CURLING ABOUT HIS LIPS. WE HOPE THAT YOU WILL HAVE THE SAME REACTION WHEN YOU TRY TODAY'S SOUP.

BALKAN BORSCHT

The recipe for this hearty root vegetable soup comes directly from "the Old Country," by way of Calgary. Make a big pot at a time, as this soup freezes well.

SERVES 8

10 cups vegetable stock or spring water
¾ cup finely diced onion
1 clove garlic, minced
2 cups peeled & diced beets
¾ cup peeled & diced celeriac
¾ cup peeled & diced parsnip
½ cup peeled & diced carrot
½ cup diced celery, stalk & leaves
2 bay leaves
Salt & pepper to taste
2 Tbsp. cider vinegar
1-2 Tbsp. honey or rice syrup

Bring stock or water to a simmer in a 6-quart pot. Add vegetables and seasonings, then simmer gently for 30 minutes.

1 cup shredded green cabbage
½ cup stemmed & shredded red or green chard

Add cabbage and chard and continue to simmer for another 15 minutes. Taste and adjust seasonings.

⅓ cup finely chopped fresh dill
½ cup finely chopped fresh parsley

Add to soup, and stir well. Serve hot.

We also suggest processing in a blender with buttermilk or soymilk to make an elegant, creamy first course.

MOONSTRUCK MINESTRONE

*Big John's version of the traditional Italian country-style
tomato soup, full of vegetables, beans and pasta. Serve it
with a salad and a crusty loaf for a complete meal.
Luciano Pavarotti, eat your heart out...*

SERVES 4

¼ cup extra virgin olive oil
1 cup diced onion
¾ cup diced celery, stalk & leaves
2 cloves garlic, minced

In a heavy-bottomed 4-quart pot, sauté the onion, celery and garlic in the oil.

1 cup skinned & chopped tomato
3 cups tomato juice
4 bay leaves
1" cinnamon stick
1 Tbsp. rice syrup or honey
1 Tbsp. cider vinegar (optional)
Salt & pepper to taste

Add tomatoes, juice and seasonings to the soup pot, and bring to a simmer over medium heat.

¾ cup diced carrot
¾ cup peeled & diced parsnip
¾ cup cauliflower florets
½ cup diced zucchini
½ cup trimmed & halved green
    beans
¾ cup stemmed & shredded swiss
    chard

Add the vegetables to the pot and simmer uncovered for 10 minutes.

¾ cup cooked chick peas (or cooked
    white beans or kidney beans)
¾ cup uncooked macaroni or small
    shell pasta
Spring water, if needed

Add beans, pasta and 1 to 2 cups extra water as needed to soup. Simmer for 10 to 15 minutes until pasta is tender.

¼ cup minced fresh basil
⅓ cup minced fresh Italian parsley
¼ cup minced fresh mint

Add herbs to soup for last 5 minutes of cooking. Serve hot.

CREAMY CURRIED CARROT SQUASH SOUP

Aromatic, piquant and definitely orange.

2-pound butternut squash, peeled &
  cubed
Spring water
3 cups peeled & cubed carrots
1 cup chopped onion
2 cloves garlic, crushed
1 cup peeled & cubed parsley root or
  celeriac
1" cinnamon stick
1 tsp. ground coriander
½ tsp. mace or nutmeg
Salt & pepper to taste

Place vegetables in a pot with water to barely cover. Bring to a boil, add spices and reduce heat to a simmer. Skim off and discard any foam that forms on the top. Simmer until vegetables are tender, then drain vegetables, reserving broth. Remove and discard bay leaves and cinnamon stick.

1 Tbsp. cashew or almond butter
2-inch piece of fresh ginger, peeled &
  grated
1 cup soymilk (if necessary)

Process the cooked vegetables in small batches in a blender or food processor, add cooking broth as necessary. Add nut butter and ginger to the last batch. When soup is all blended, thin with soymilk if needed.

1 bunch fresh cilantro or
fennel fronds or parsley, finely
  chopped

Add the fresh herbs to soup and reheat gently, stirring often.

BRAZILIAN BLACK BEAN SOUP

This fragrant soup is spicy and seductive, with the tang of orange and a hint of heat. Serve it with rice and a salad.

SERVES 4

2 cups dried black turtle beans,
    sorted, rinsed & soaked
    overnight in
4 cups spring water
1" cinnamon stick
1 dried hot chili pod
1 small whole orange, rinsed
1 bay leaf

In a 4-quart pot, bring the beans in their soaking liquid to a boil. Add spices and orange, reduce heat and simmer for about 2 hours, or until beans are tender, adding more water if needed. Remove and discard spices and orange. Set aside 2 cups of cooked beans and liquid, leaving the rest in the pot over low heat.

¼ cup sunflower oil
1 cup diced onion
¾ cup diced celery
½ cup diced red bell peppers
½ cup diced yellow mild peppers
1 small hot fresh pepper, seeded &
    minced
4 cloves garlic, minced
2 Tbsp. ground cumin
1 Tbsp. dried basil
Salt & pepper to taste

In a skillet, heat oil and sauté the onion and celery for 5 minutes. Add the peppers, garlic and herbs, and saute for 5 more minutes. Add to the beans in the soup pot.

2 medium seedless oranges, zest &
    flesh
1 can (14 oz.) hearts of palm, drained
    & sliced in ¼" rounds
½ cup finely diced parsley

Zest the oranges, then trim white layer away. Cut the trimmed oranges into bite-sized pieces and add along with zest to soup. Add hearts of palm and parsley, stir well, and adjust seasoning. Purée reserved beans and liquid in a blender or food processor, then add to soup to thicken it. Stir well and simmer for 10 minutes. Serve hot.

BRAZILIAN BLACK BEAN SOUP

This soup beats with the pulse of Brazil — black beans, fresh oranges, hearts of palm, peppers, onions, garlic, cumin, cinnamon — delicious and exotic, like the dream-like world of a Jorge Amado novel.

CORN CHOWDER

Soymilk works beautifully as the base for this fast and delicious soup.
Serve with corn bread and Lemon Broccoli, page 41 .

Serve with corn bread and Lemon Broccoli, page 41 .

SERVES 4

2 cups unpeeled, cubed red potatoes
4 cups spring water
½ tsp. salt (optional)

Bring (salted) water to a rolling boil in a 2-quart pot. Add potatoes and cook until tender. Do not overcook. Remove from heat, drain and reserve liquid. Return potatoes to pot and set aside.

2 cups finely chopped onions
1 cup finely chopped celery
6 diced green onions
3 Tbsp. corn oil
3 Tbsp. minced fresh tarragon
1½ Tbsp. minced fresh marjoram

In a skillet, heat oil and sauté vegetables with herbs until tender but not brown. Add to potatoes.

4 cups soymilk
2 cups reserved cooking liquid or
    stock
⅓ cup chopped fresh parsley
3 cups corn kernels
Salt & pepper to taste

Add to potatoes and stir well. Heat gently over medium heat, stirring often, making certain it does not boil.

CLASSIC SPLIT PEA SOUP

A favourite fall soup that is hearty and comforting.

SERVES 4

6 cups spring water
1 cup dried green split peas
5-6 crushed black pepper-corns
2 bay leaves

Bring water to a boil in a 4-quart pot. Rinse the split peas and place immediately into boiling water with spices and stir. Reduce heat and simmer for about an hour until they are very tender. Skim off and discard any foam that forms during cooking. Remove from heat and discard bay leaves.

1 cup diced onions
½ tsp. dried sage
1 Tbsp. dried thyme
¼ cup virgin olive oil

Sauté onions and herbs in oil until lightly browned. Add to split peas and process in blender or food processor until smooth. Return to soup pot.

6 cups spring water
1 tsp. salt (optional)
2 cups peeled & diced potatoes
1 cup peeled & thinly sliced carrots
1 cup diced celery

Bring (salted) water to a boil in a 2-quart pot. Add vegetables and boil until just tender. Drain and discard water, add vegetables to soup pot.

2-3 Tbsp. tamari
Black pepper to taste
¼ cup sherry (optional)

Add to soup and stir well. Heat gently, continuing to stir. Do not let boil.

YELLOW SPLIT PEA DAHL

This beautiful yellow soup is easy to prepare and blends the subtle,
mysterious flavours of India. Serve with chapatis
and a vegetable curry.

SERVES 4

10 cups spring water
2 cups yellow split peas

Place water in a heavy-bottomed pot. Rinse split peas and place immediately in the pot; bring water to a boil. Reduce heat and simmer uncovered for 45-60 minutes, until peas are soft and breaking apart. Skim off and discard any foam that forms while cooking.

¼ cup almond or sunflower oil
1 cup diced onion
4 cloves garlic, minced
2 tsp. curry powder
2 tsp. ground cumin
½ tsp. garam masala
1 cup diced red bell pepper
1 cup diced green bell pepper

Heat oil in a wok or skillet. Add onions, garlic and spices and sauté over medium high heat until onions are browned — about 10 minutes. Add the peppers for the last five minutes of cooking. Add all to cooked peas.

1 tsp. ground coriander
½ tsp. ground fennel
¼ tsp. cardamom
¼ tsp. cinnamon
½ tsp. cayenne
Salt to taste
¼ cup lemon juice

Add spices and lemon juice to the soup, stir well and simmer over low heat for 15 to 20 minutes. Serve hot. The flavour of this soup improves from sitting overnight in the refrigerator. Reheat gently before serving.

VEGETARIAN CHILI

*The recipe for this crowd pleaser comes straight
from Texas. Make it hot enough to put a little fire
into February and serve it with salad and corn bread.*

SERVES 4

1 cup pinto beans, sorted, rinsed &
    soaked overnight in
3 cups spring water
½" cinnamon stick
2 cloves garlic, minced
1 dried hot pepper
1 tsp. black pepper

Bring beans and soaking water to a boil in heavy-bottomed pan. Add spices, reduce heat and simmer until beans are well done – approximately 3 hours, adding more water as needed. Remove and discard cinnamon stick and pepper pod.

3 Tbsp. corn oil
2 tsp. cumin seeds
1 cup chopped onion
½ cup chopped green bell pepper
2 Tbsp. chili powder
2 tsp. ground coriander
4 drops Tabasco sauce (or more, to
    taste)
Black pepper to taste

Heat oil and sauté cumin seeds. Add onions, peppers and spices and cook until onions are browned. Add to beans.

1 (14 oz.) can tomatoes, with juice
¼ cup bulgur wheat
1 cup corn kernels
4 Tbsp. tamari
1 (4 oz.) can diced green chilis

Chop up tomatoes. Add tomatoes, juice and bulgur wheat to chili pot. Simmer over low heat for 20 minutes. Stir well and frequently to prevent scorching. Add corn, tamari and chilis and cook, stirring, for 15 minutes longer.

Viva Terlingua Chili

Jerry Jeff Walker, outlaw musician, has an album called "Viva Terlingua" in honour of a Texas ghost town, where Mexico is as close as a shallow crossing of the Rio Grande. Normally the desert silence is broken only by the howls of coyotes, but once a year folks from all over gather for an awesome chili cook-off. In the spirit of Terlingua, we offer you a vegetarian chili that is a perfect antidote for a cool, rainy Canadian day. Make it as hot as you can stand, and then some ...

CREAMY ASPARAGUS SOUP

*A springtime green soup, with a delicate
yet sturdy base of celeriac.*

SERVES 4

1 pound asparagus, trimmed &
    peeled as needed

Cut the asparagus into 1" lengths.
Set aside stems to add to soup pot.
Lightly steam the tips separately
and set aside.

5-6 cups spring water
4 cups peeled & diced celeriac
1 cup diced onion
½ cup finely diced celery, stalk &
    leaves
2 bay leaves
Salt & pepper to taste

Bring water to boil in a 3-quart pot.
Add vegetables (including asparagus
stems) and seasonings. Lower heat
and simmer gently until celeriac is
very tender (15 to 20 minutes).

When the vegetables are tender,
remove from heat and drain,
reserving stock. Remove bay leaves
and purée the vegetables in a
blender or food processor, adding
stock as needed to reach desired
consistency.

1 cup soymilk
½ cup minced fresh parsley
3 Tbsp. minced fresh chervil,
    tarragon or chives

Place hot blended soup in pot or
tureen and stir in soymilk and herbs
until well-blended. Add steamed
asparagus tips, stir gently. Serve
hot. Reheat gently if necessary over
low heat, but do not let boil.

CORN AND CILANTRO GAZPACHO

Fresh and flavourful, this no-cook summer soup is best when made 4 to 24 hours ahead to let the flavours blend. Serve with refried beans, guacamole and corn tortilla chips.

SERVES 4

4 cups tomato juice

Chill.

1 cup frozen corn kernels, thawed
1 cup peeled & finely diced jicama
½ cup finely diced green onion
½ cup finely diced red bell pepper
½ cup finely diced green bell pepper
1 cup finely diced cucumber
1 fresh jalapeno or serrano pepper,
    seeded & minced
¼ cup minced fresh cilantro
¼ cup lime juice
1 tsp. lime zest
Black pepper to taste
¼ cup Tequila or white rum
    (optional)

Add to the tomato juice. Stir well, cover and chill. Serve cool from a chilled tureen.

ROASTED PUMPKIN AND GARLIC SOUP

*This is a luscious, autumnal orange soup. Serve with
a spinach salad and Maple Piñon Muffins, page 93.*

SERVES 4

4-pound pumpkin
4 large cloves garlic, peeled

PREHEAT OVEN TO 400 DEGREES F.
Cut pumpkin in half. Remove and
discard the seeds and stringy fibres.
Turn halves upside down over
peeled garlic cloves, onto an oiled
pan with a rim. Roast for an hour
(or more) until pumpkin flesh
mashes easily with a fork all the way
through to the skin. Scoop out the
cooked flesh and discard the skin.

½ tsp. dried sage
Salt & pepper to taste
3-4 cups soymilk

In a food processor or blender,
blend pumpkin, garlic and spices,
adding enough soymilk to reach the
desired consistency.
Return to pot and heat gently while
stirring. Do not let it boil.

SALADS AND SIDE DISHES

These are the recipes that we would nominate for Best Supporting Salad if they gave out Oscars for meals...veteran performers good enough to steal the show from a main dish, especially these days when fewer people are basing a meal on meat. Our salads (to be served cold) and side dishes (to be savoured hot) are vibrant, colourful collections of vegetables and grains, with tangy dressings to intrigue and tantalize. Serve them with vegetarian entrées, or in combination with other salads. They are prize winners one and all. 🥀

LEMON BROCCOLI

*This broccoli salad makes a great accompaniment,
quick to make and pretty to look at.*

1 large head broccoli
6 cups spring water

Cut the broccoli tops into bite-sized flowers. Discard bottom 1 to 2 inches of stem, peel the rest of stem and slice into 2-inch sticks. Bring the water to a boil, add broccoli and blanch for 2 minutes, then plunge broccoli immediately into cold water to stop cooking process. Drain thoroughly.

3 Tbsp. lemon juice
3 Tbsp. minced fresh mint (or basil or fennel — use only fresh herbs, not dried)
1 tsp. honey
2 Tbsp. pine nuts
Salt to taste

Process briefly in a food processor until well blended. If working by hand, mince herbs and pine nuts then mix vigorously.

⅓ cup light virgin olive oil

With processor running, trickle in oil in a steady stream to emulsify dressing. By hand, trickle in while whisking vigorously.
In clean dry bowl, toss broccoli with dressing to coat.

½ lemon, halved & very thinly sliced
2 Tbsp. pine nuts

Add to broccoli and toss gently. Serve at room temperature.

SEA SALAD

*This mineral-rich salad presents itself beautifully.
It has long been a favourite at The Big Carrot deli.*

SERVES 4

1 cup dried arame
½ cup dried hijiki

Rinse the dried sea vegetables well. Place them in large pot of cold water and bring to a boil. Let boil for 5 minutes, remove from heat and let stand, covered, for 3 to 4 hours in the cooking water, so that vegetables can rehydrate. Drain well. Rinse again, if desired, for a milder flavour.

¼ cup finely diced red bell pepper
½ cup finely diced green bell pepper
¼ cup finely diced green onion
¼ cup coarsely chopped fresh parsley
¼ cup corn kernels
½ Tbsp. safflower oil
2 Tbsp. lemon juice
1 Tbsp. tamari

Add to the cooked sea vegetables and toss well.

CORN AND JICAMA RELISH

Featuring cool and crispy jicama, this colourful Mexican relish makes a great summer side dish.

SERVES 4

2 cups corn kernels, blanched
½ cup finely diced red bell pepper
1½ cups peeled & finely diced jicama
¼ cup fresh lime juice
¼ cup finely diced green onion
¼ cup diced fresh cilantro
¼ cup diced fresh parsley
2 cloves garlic, minced
1 Tbsp. corn oil
1 Tbsp. picante sauce (not Tabasco
    style; see Glossary)
Salt & pepper to taste

Toss all ingredients together in a mixing bowl. Refrigerate for at least one to two hours before serving.

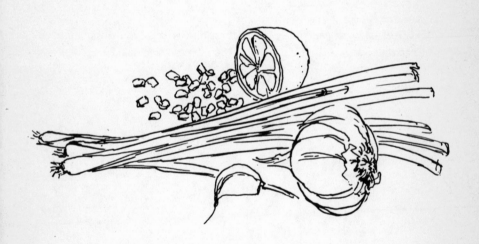

LOVELY LICORICE SALAD

*A light summer salad with the taste of anise —
as elegant as it is quick to prepare.*

SERVES 4

3 small navel oranges
Bed of mixed greens: spinach, Boston
or Romaine lettuce, radicchio,
watercress, etc., stemmed, rinsed
& drained
1 English cucumber, cut into ¼"
thick rounds

Grate orange peel; set aside. Slice oranges into ¼ inch thick rounds. On platter or individual salad plates, create a bed of salad greens. Arrange cucumber and orange slices on top of greens.

1 Tbsp. aniseed
¼ cup walnut pieces, toasted
Zest from 3 oranges (above)
Freshly ground black pepper to taste

Scatter over composed salad.

1 Tbsp. lemon juice
1 Tbsp. rice syrup or honey
¼ cup sunflower or walnut oil

Combine with a fork in a small bowl then drizzle over salad.

CABBAGE AND CRESS SALAD

Vivid colours and a tangy citrus dressing make this cabbage salad a summer delight.

SERVES 4

3 cups shredded red cabbage

Soak shredded cabbage in very cold water. Drain just before tossing salad.

½ cup thinly sliced red radishes
½ cup peeled & julienned daikon radish
1 bunch watercress, rinsed & stemmed

Soak radishes and cress in very cold water, separately from cabbage so they won't pick up colour.

1 cup hazelnuts

Toast the hazelnuts in 400 degree F oven for 10 minutes. Let cool and rub to remove skins. Set aside ⅓ cup nuts for dressing.

¼ cup grapefruit juice
1 Tbsp. rice syrup or honey
½ tsp. grated fresh ginger
Salt & pepper to taste
1 Tbsp. toasted sesame oil
⅓ cup canola or sunflower oil

In blender or food processor, blend ⅓ cup toasted hazelnuts with dressing ingredients until smooth, trickling oil in at the end in a steady stream until dressing emulsifies. (If working by hand, whisk vigorously until dressing thickens.)

¼ cup black sesame seeds

Drain cabbage, radishes and cress well. In a large salad bowl, toss with hazelnuts, dressing and sesame seeds. Serve immediately.

SPICY TEX-MEX RICE

You will find this style of rice in Mexican restaurants all over Texas, usually alongside refried beans. Serve with enchiladas, tacos, or burritos.

SERVES 4

1½ scant cups spring water
½ tsp. salt (optional)
¾ cup long grain brown rice

Bring (salted) water to boil in a heavy-bottomed 2-quart pot with lid. Add rice, return to a boil, then reduce heat to simmer. Simmer, covered, over low heat for about 45 minutes or until rice is tender but not mushy. Remove from heat and let stand covered to retain warmth.

¼ cup lime juice

Pour over the cooked rice.

4 Tbsp. corn oil or
other light vegetable oil
½ tsp. dried crushed hot chilis

Heat the oil in a skillet or wok. Add the dried chilis. Cook for 3 to 4 minutes over medium heat.

½ cup peeled & finely diced carrot
½ cup finely diced onion
½ cup finely diced celery
¼ cup finely diced green onion
½ cup corn kernels
2 cloves garlic, minced

Add the carrots, onions and celery to the hot oil and sauté for 5 minutes. Then add green onions, garlic and corn, sautéeing for 2 minutes more.

1 cup chopped canned tomatoes, with
    juice
¼ cup chopped fresh cilantro leaves
1 tsp. ground cumin
1 tsp. chili powder
2 – 4 Tbsp. picante
sauce (adjust to taste. Do not use
    Tabasco style — see Glossary)
Salt & pepper to taste

Add to sautéed vegetables, reduce heat and simmer until heated through. Add to cooked rice and stir thoroughly. Serve warm.

BROWN RICE AND ADUKI BEAN SALAD

*This colourful dish of rice and beans makes a complete
protein and is savoury served hot or cold.*

SERVES 4

1¼ cups spring water
¾ cup brown basmati rice
1 Tbsp. miso

Bring water to a boil in a 1-quart pot. Add rice and miso, return to a boil, then reduce heat and simmer, covered, for 45 minutes or until rice is completely cooked.

2 Tbsp. sesame oil
1 Tbsp. grated fresh ginger
2 cloves garlic, minced
⅓ cup finely diced carrot
⅓ cup finely diced celery
⅓ cup finely diced red bell pepper
⅓ cup finely diced leek (optional)

Heat oil. Add garlic and ginger, then sauté for one minute. Add vegetables and sauté for 4 to 5 minutes. Add to rice.

1 cup cooked aduki beans
½ cup diced green onions
2 Tbsp. diced cilantro

Add to rice.

1 Tbsp. rice vinegar
1 Tbsp. rice syrup
2 Tbsp. tamari
1 Tbsp. toasted sesame oil
1 Tbsp. black sesame
seeds (or use toasted)
½ tsp. mirin
1 Tbsp. water

Mix together in a small bowl until thoroughly blended. Add to rice and vegetables and toss thoroughly.

QUINOA SALAD

*An ancient grain cultivated by the Aztecs, quinoa makes
a nutritious foundation for this light and tasty salad.*

SERVES 4

1 cup quinoa, rinsed
1¾ cups spring water

Bring water to a boil in a 1-quart pot, then add quinoa. Reduce heat and simmer covered for 15 minutes, stirring occasionally until grain is tender. Remove from heat and let cool uncovered.

½ cup finely diced English cucumber
4 stems finely diced green onion
¼ cup finely diced fresh cilantro
⅓ cup corn kernels

Toss with cooked quinoa.

3 Tbsp. fresh lime juice
3 Tbsp. sesame oil
1 Tbsp. toasted sesame oil
Salt & pepper to taste
1 tsp. rice syrup or honey (optional)

Combine, then add to quinoa. Stir thoroughly with a fork to coat grain and vegetables.

TABOULI

This light and quick-to-prepare salad is popular throughout the Middle East. Serve on a bed of lettuce, with hummus and pita bread for a zesty summer meal.

SERVES 4

1 cup raw bulgur wheat
½ tsp. salt (optional)
1¼ cups boiling water

Place bulgur (and salt) in a bowl. Pour boiling water over the wheat and stir well. Set aside for 30 minutes, stirring occasionally, until water is completely absorbed and the bulgur is tender.

¼ cup chopped fresh mint
¼ cup chopped fresh parsley
1 cup diced English cucumber
1 cup diced tomato
½ cup diced red onion

Add to the cooked bulgur and stir well.

2 cloves garlic, minced
¼ cup lemon juice
¼ cup virgin olive oil
3-4 drops Tabasco sauce
Salt & pepper to taste

Mix dressing ingredients well in a small bowl. Pour over bulgur and toss well. Best when allowed to stand and cool for several hours.

TROPICAL POTATO SALAD

A deliciously different potato salad

SERVES 4

4 cups peeled & cubed potatoes
6 cups spring water
1 tsp. salt (optional)

Bring (salted) water to a boil in a 4 quart pot. Add potatoes and boil until tender but not mushy. Rinse with cold water to stop cooking process. Drain well and place in a large bowl.

1 cup sliced carrots, blanched
1 cup peas, blanched
4 red radishes, thinly sliced
2 stalks celery, sliced
1 cup quartered & sliced English
    cucumber
2 Tbsp. sunflower seeds

Add to the cooked potatoes.

¼ cup lemon juice
½ cup sesame oil
1 Tbsp. honey
2 cloves garlic
2-3 drops Tabasco sauce
½ cup shredded coconut
3 Tbsp. fresh parsley
Salt & pepper to taste

Combine in a blender or food processor, then pour this dressing over the potatoes. Toss gently.

½ cup roasted soybeans

Add to potato salad just before serving, to preserve crunchiness.

DILLED POTATO SALAD

When the first new red potatoes and fresh dill appear in the markets, make this salad and rejoice. This summery salad is perfect for picnics.

SERVES 4

4 cups scrubbed & cubed (1" cubes)
    red new potatoes
6 cups spring water
½ tsp. salt (optional)

In a 3-quart pot, bring (salted) water to a boil. Add potatoes and cook for 15 to 20 minutes until just tender. Drain and place in a mixing bowl.

1 cup sliced green bell pepper
½ cup diagonally diced green onions
1 cup cubed English cucumbers

Add peppers, green onions and cucumbers to cooked potatoes.

⅓ cup minced fresh dill
¼ cup cider vinegar
1½ Tbsp. Dijon mustard
Salt & pepper to taste
½ tsp. honey or rice syrup
½ cup sunflower oil

In a bowl or blender, mix dill, vinegar and seasonings. Trickle oil in slowly while blending or whisking vigorously, until dressing is thick and smooth. Pour over potatoes and toss gently but thoroughly. Serve at room temperature.

DÜSSELDORF POTATOES

A delicious dairy-free rendition of scalloped potatoes, with a rich mustard sauce.

SERVES 8

7 large potatoes, scrubbed
10 cups spring water

Place water in a 6-quart pot. Add whole potatoes and bring to a boil over medium-high heat. Cook until tender, about 40 minutes. Drain and plunge into cold water for one minute, drain again, then allow to sit until thoroughly cooled. Peel if desired. Slice in ¼-inch-thick rounds.

¼ cup sunflower oil
1½ cups finely chopped onions
1 tsp. turmeric
⅓ cup rye or whole wheat flour
2 Tbsp. miso (light barley or rice)
2⅔ cups spring water
⅔ cup plain soymilk
¼ cup mild Dijon mustard
2 Tbsp. tahini
¼ cup snipped chives,
dried or fresh (or finely diced green onions)
Salt & pepper to taste

PREHEAT OVEN TO 375 DEGREES F.

Sauté onions and turmeric in oil in a heavy-bottomed saucepan until translucent. Stir in flour and blend well, then cook for 2 minutes over medium heat. Mix water and miso in a small bowl to make a broth. Whisk miso broth into onions, stirring constantly. Reduce heat and whisk in soymilk, mustard and tahini. Season to taste with chives, salt and pepper. Simmer, stirring and reducing until thick but still pourable.

CONTINUED

1 cup bread crumbs

Lightly oil a 9"x13" glass casserole pan and layer half the sliced potatoes evenly on the bottom. Pour half the sauce over them and repeat with remainder of potatoes and sauce. Sprinkle top with bread crumbs. Bake at 375 degrees for 25 minutes, or until casserole is bubbling and bread crumbs are browned. Serve hot.

ENTREES

Hot or cold, winter or summer, the entrée is the foundation on which rests the success of a meal; the heart, the very soul of a plate set before you. So it had better be good...appealing, wonderful and full of nutrition. Some entrées are meant to be exotic and seductive; at other times, dinner needs to be as comfortable and welcoming as your favourite rocking chair.

We have included a selection of dishes from around the world, from eastern Europe to the Eastern Townships, Italy to Indonesia, Amarillo to Asia. At the front of this section, you'll find dishes that are meant to be served at room temperature; appealing textures and colours to suit a summer table and get you through the heat. Later come the warm, aromatic, bubbling, piping, filling mainstays for autumn and winter. You'll encounter both new flavours and old favourites from childhood. Everything from the sublime to the familiar...

SINGAPORE SOBA SALAD

*An exotic main dish salad of soba noodles and vegetables,
eaten cold with a spicy peanut dressing.
Serve on a bed of lettuce with cucumber slices.*

SERVES 4

8 ounces dried soba noodles
6 cups spring water

Bring water to a rolling boil in a 4-quart pot. Break soba noodles in half and drop into boiling water over medium high heat. Cook using "shock" method described on page 18, until the noodles are cooked to desired tenderness. Drain and rinse immediately with cold water, draining again well. Place cooked noodles in a large bowl.

2 Tbsp. sesame oil
½ cup julienned red bell pepper
¾ cup julienned green bell pepper
1 cup julienned carrots

In a wok, heat oil and stir fry peppers and carrots over high heat for 2 minutes. Add to noodles.

2 cups shredded bok choy or Napa
    cabbage
⅓ cup black Japanese sesame seeds
    (or toasted sesame seeds)
⅓ cup finely diced green onions

Add to cooked noodles.

½ cup smooth peanut butter
2 Tbsp. tahini
¼ cup warm water
⅓ cup rice wine vinegar
¼ cup tamari
2 Tbsp. rice syrup (or honey)
2 tsp. hot picante or chili sauce

Process in blender or food processor until well mixed. Pour over noodles and vegetables. Toss the salad until mixed and all ingredients are coated with dressing. Top with additional black sesame seeds for decoration.

PASTA ROMA

*This colourful pasta salad with the taste of balsamic vinegar
makes a perfect summer meal. Serve on a bed of Romaine lettuce
with sliced ripe tomatoes.*

SERVES 4

6 cups spring water
1 tsp. salt (optional)
3 cups uncooked pasta spirals or
    shells

Bring (salted) water to a rolling boil in a 3-quart pot. Add pasta and cook until al dente, stirring occasionally. Drain. Rinse in cold water and drain again. Transfer to a large bowl.

½ cup julienned red bell peppers
½ cup julienned green bell peppers
½ cup thinly sliced red onion
½ cup julienned carrots, blanched
½ cup pitted Calamata black olives

Add to cooked noodles.

1 Tbsp. dried basil
⅓ cup lemon juice
2 cloves garlic
2 Tbsp. capers
½ tsp. grated nutmeg
1½ Tbsp. balsamic vinegar
Salt & pepper to taste

Combine in a food processor or blender until garlic is minced. If working by hand, mince garlic and capers first, then combine all in a small bowl.

½ cup light virgin olive oil

With processor running, trickle in oil until dressing emulsifies. If working by hand, whisk vigorously while adding oil.

Toss all ingredients together until well mixed. Serve at room temperature.

GOI GA VIETNAMESE SALAD

This fresh and crunchy salad with spicy-hot dressing is at its best when served fresh. Herbert Pryke, our consulting chef, brought this recipe direct from Asia.

SERVES 4

2 cups spring water
½ tsp. salt (optional)
1 cup brown basmati rice

Bring (salted) water to a boil in 1-quart pot with a lid. Add rice, return to a boil, then reduce heat and simmer, covered, for 45 minutes until rice is tender. Set aside and allow to cool completely.

½ cup thinly sliced red onion
1 cup julienned carrots
½ cup julienned red bell pepper
½ cup julienned green bell pepper
5 red radishes, thinly sliced
1 packed cup fresh spinach, rinsed, stemmed & cut in a chiffonade (see page 17)
2 packed cups Boston lettuce leaves, rinsed & cut in a chiffonade
2½ cups roasted peanuts
1 cup bean sprouts

Mix well with cooled rice in a large bowl.

3 Tbsp. tamari
3 Tbsp. cider vinegar
1 dried hot chili pepper, boiled for 5 minutes to soften, drained & minced
1 Tbsp. lemon juice
1 tsp. rice syrup or honey

Mix the dressing, then toss gently with the salad. Refrigerate to chill, and serve within 1 to 2 hours of preparing.

TOFU PASTA SALAD

*A cool and creamy pasta salad with highlights of mustard and garlic.
This recipe was developed by Sarah Ayerst,
an expert in working with soyfoods.*

SERVES 4

4 cups dried spiral pasta
8 cups water
1 tsp. salt (optional)

Bring (salted) water to a rolling boil in a 4-quart pot. Add pasta, then boil for 10 to 12 minutes, stirring occasionally until al dente. Drain, rinse immediately with cold water and drain well again.

1 cup diagonally sliced celery
½ cup diagonally sliced green onion
½ cup chopped parsley
2 cups peeled & grated carrots

Add to the cooked pasta in a large bowl and mix well.

½ cup plain soymilk
2 tsp. Dijon mustard
1 Tbsp. lemon juice
1 large clove garlic
Salt & pepper to taste

Process in food processor or blender until garlic is finely chopped.

½ cup soy oil

With machine running, trickle oil in slowly to emulsify dressing. Add to pasta and stir well to coat.

1 block tofu, pressed & drained

Cut into ½-inch cubes. Add to pasta salad and toss gently. Serve at room temperature.

MILLET FLORENTINE

An elegant casserole of golden millet topped
with a spinach-mushroom sauté and toasted almonds.

SERVES 8

3 cups spring water
1 tsp. salt (optional)
1½ cups raw millet

PREHEAT OVEN TO 350 DEGREES F.
Bring (salted) water to a boil in a 2-quart pot. Rinse the millet well, drain and add to boiling water. Reduce heat and simmer uncovered for 20 to 30 minutes, stirring often, until millet is dry and tender. Remove from heat and place in a mixing bowl.

1 cup peeled & grated carrot
4 cloves garlic, minced
½ Tbsp. dried marjoram
1½ cubes tofu, pressed & drained

Add the carrots, garlic and marjoram to the millet. Crumble the tofu, then add to the millet, stirring well until thoroughly mixed. Place in an oiled 9 x 13 inch casserole pan, and pat level with a rubber spatula. Bake uncovered for 20 minutes. Remove and set aside.

2 Tbsp. sunflower oil
1½ cups diced onions
2 cups sliced mushrooms

In a skillet, heat the oil over medium heat and sauté the onions for 5 minutes. Add mushrooms, and continue to sauté for 5 more minutes.

1 (10-oz. bag) fresh spinach, well
    rinsed, stemmed & coarsely
    chopped
½ cup slivered or sliced almonds
½ cup finely diced red bell pepper
½ Tbsp. ground nutmeg
Salt & pepper to taste
3 Tbsp. lemon juice
2-3 Tbsp. arrowroot powder

Add the chopped spinach, almonds, red pepper and seasonings to the skillet along with the lemon juice. Reduce heat to low and simmer for 4 to 5 minutes, stirring often. Sprinkle on arrowroot, stirring and simmering until liquid from cooking is absorbed. Remove from heat. Spread evenly over baked

CONTINUED

¼ cup slivered or sliced almonds

millet to form top layer of casserole. Sprinkle with almonds and return to oven for 10 minutes, until nuts are toasted. Serve hot.

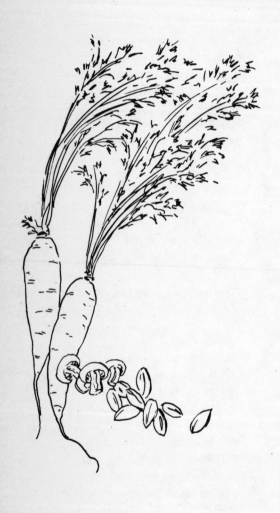

EGGPLANT PARMESAN

A classic Italian vegetarian favourite featuring polenta and baked — not fried! — eggplant, seasoned with herbs. So delicious that even people who don't like eggplant may like this dish.

SERVES 8

5-6 cups spring water
2 cups cornmeal
1 tsp. dried oregano
½ tsp. black pepper
1 tsp. thyme
Salt to taste

Bring water to a boil in a heavy-bottomed pot. Whisk in cornmeal and spices, reduce heat and simmer for 20 to 30 minutes until cornmeal is tender, stirring often. This polenta should be thin and easily spreadable; whisk in more water if needed. Remove from heat.

1 cup grated mozzarella cheese
¼ cup Parmesan cheese

Stir cheeses into the polenta and set aside to cool.

2½ lbs. eggplant
Olive oil
Salt & pepper to taste
1-2 Tbsp. dried basil

PREHEAT OVEN TO 425 DEGREES F. Rinse eggplants and slice into ½-inch-thick rounds. Place on oiled cookie sheet, lightly brush oil on tops and sprinkle with spices. Bake for 20 minutes or until well browned. Remove from oven and REDUCE HEAT TO 325 DEGREES.

Olive oil
1 cup tomato sauce
2 cups grated mozzarella cheese

Lightly oil a 9"x13" casserole pan. Spread ⅓ cup tomato sauce evenly over the bottom of the dish. Place half the eggplant slices in the tomato sauce. Spoon half the polenta on top, using a rubber spatula to evenly spread mixture. Sprinkle with half of mozzarella cheese. Repeat this layering process with ⅓ cup tomato sauce and the rest of the eggplant and polenta.

CONTINUED

Top with remaining tomato sauce and mozzarella. Bake at 325 degrees for 20 minutes.

⅓ cup Parmesan cheese

Sprinkle with Parmesan cheese and bake 10 minutes more. Serve hot.

LASAGNE MEDITERRANEE A PESTO

*Like many of the finer things in life, lasagne is a lot of work.
This recipe is no exception, but the pesto and roasted peppers
make it well worth the effort.*

SERVES 8

3 large green or red bell peppers, cut
in half lengthwise & seeded

PREHEAT OVEN TO 500 DEGREES F.
Place pepper halves on oiled baking
sheet, cut side down, and roast until
skins are blackened and blistered.
Remove from oven and cover with a
tea towel for 5 minutes until cool
enough to handle. Remove and
discard skins, then set peppers
aside. REDUCE OVEN TO 350 DEGREES.

1½ lbs. zucchini
Pesto (a bottled variety or use recipe
on page 127)

Slice zucchini into ¼-inch-thick
rounds and place on oiled baking
sheet. Baste with pesto and bake at
350 degrees for about 20 minutes,
until tender. Remove from oven and
set aside. Leave oven at 350 degrees.

2 cups (16 oz.) cottage or ricotta
cheese
½ cup grated Parmesan or Swiss
Sbrinz cheese
2 eggs
½ tsp. nutmeg

Blend cottage cheese in food
processor or food mill until it is
smooth. Mix with Parmesan, eggs
and nutmeg. Set aside.

2 large tomatoes, thinly sliced
2 cups grated mozzarella cheese
4 cups tomato sauce
4 oz. can roasted mild green chilis,
drained (optional)
8 oz. fresh or dried lasagna noodles

Clear the decks for action and
gather all ingredients for assembly.

In a 9"x13" casserole pan, assemble
lasagne in the following order.

CONTINUED

Spread evenly over the bottom of the pan:
¾ cup tomato sauce
1 layer of pasta
¾ cup tomato sauce
Zucchini with pesto
Half of the cottage cheese mix
¾ cup tomato sauce
Half of the grated mozzarella cheese
1 layer of pasta
¾ cup tomato sauce
Roasted peppers and chilis
Tomato slices
Last half of cottage cheese mix
1 layer of pasta
¾ cup tomato sauce

And top with last half of grated mozzarella cheese

Bake in a 350 degree F oven for 30 minutes until bubbly and browned. Serve hot.

SHEPHERD'S PIE

A delicious vegetarian version of the traditional
country casserole topped with creamy mashed potatoes.

SERVES 8

⅔ cup rye, barley or wheat flour
⅓ cup soy oil
2 tsp. honey

In a heavy-bottomed 1-quart pot, combine flour, oil and honey over medium-high heat, stirring constantly with a fork or whisk. Cook this smooth paste for 5 to 10 minutes until browned.

2 cups tomato juice
3 Tbsp. tomato paste
2 tsp. cider vinegar
2 tsp. dried thyme
½ tsp. dried sage
Salt and pepper to taste
Water if needed

Slowly whisk in tomato juice, paste, vinegar and spices. Lower heat to medium and continue to cook for 5 more minutes, stirring constantly to form a thick sauce. Add water if necessary. Set aside.

3 cups chopped onions
1 cup chopped carrot
4 cups mushroom halves
¼ cup soy oil

Sauté onions and carrots in oil in a skillet for 5 minutes. Add mushrooms and continue to sauté for 5 more minutes or until vegetables are just tender.

1 cup peas
1 cup chopped green beans
2 cubes tofu, pressed, drained & cut
   in ¾" cubes

Combine peas, beans and tofu with sautéed onions in a large bowl. Add tomato sauce, stirring gently and thoroughly. Spread in an even layer in bottom of an oiled 9" x 13" casserole pan.
PREHEAT OVEN TO 300 DEGREES F.

CONTINUED

2½ lbs. potatoes, peeled & cubed
⅓ cup soymilk
2 Tbsp. soy oil
⅓ tsp. paprika
⅓ tsp. turmeric
3 Tbsp. minced chives or parsley

Boil potatoes in salted water for 15 to 20 minutes until tender. Drain and mash with soymilk, oil and spices until smooth and creamy. Spread evenly on top of vegetable filling in casserole.

Smooth flat with a spatula, then use the tines of a fork to etch ridges in a decorative design in the potatoes. Bake, uncovered, for 20 to 30 minutes until lightly browned.

TOFU POT PIE

A new version of a childhood favourite, this vegetarian pot pie uses tofu as the base, with a rich brown gravy and plenty of vegetables.

MAKES ONE 9 INCH PIE, SERVES 6

---

1 block tofu, pressed & drained
2 Tbsp. tamari
Corn oil

PREHEAT OVEN TO 425 DEGREES F.
Cut tofu into 3/4" cubes. In a small bowl, gently toss with tamari, then spread on oiled cookie sheet and bake for 15 minutes until brown and crispy. Remove from oven and REDUCE OVEN HEAT TO 350 DEGREES.

5 cups spring water
1 tsp. salt (optional)
1 cup peeled & cubed potatoes
¾ cup cubed carrots
¾ cup cubed parsnip or turnip

Bring water to a rolling boil in a 3-quart pot. Add the potatoes and boil for 10 minutes, then add carrots and parsnips and boil for 5 to 10 more minutes until vegetables are barely tender. Do not overcook. Drain and place in a large bowl.

1 cup chopped onions
1 Tbsp. corn oil

Sauté the onions in the oil until translucent. Add to the cooked vegetables.

½ cup chopped celery
½ cup frozen peas

Add to the cooked vegetables.

1 Tbsp. corn oil
¼ cup tahini
½ cup engevita or nutritional yeast
   (not baking yeast)
4 Tbsp. tamari
¼ cup unbleached white flour
2 tsp. basil
Black pepper to taste
1 tsp. ground rosemary
2 tsp. dried ground sage
1 bay leaf

In a heavy-bottomed saucepan over medium heat, whisk oil, tahini, yeast, tamari and flour together to form a smooth paste. Whisk in herbs and simmer for 5 minutes, stirring often.

CONTINUED

2½ cups spring water or vegetable stock

Whisk in water to form a gravy, then boil for 10 minutes to thicken, stirring often. Remove from heat and pour over cooked vegetables. Stir gently but thoroughly.

Pastry — see page 99.

Roll out the pastry into 2 even circles to fit a 9-inch pie plate. Line the plate with one circle of dough. Fill with vegetables and gravy. Place the second circle of pastry to form a top layer. Seal, trim and crimp the edges of the two layers of pastry, using a fork or your fingers. Using a sharp knife, gently cut an x or other shape into centre of the top crust to allow steam to escape. If you have extra pastry, decorate the top with leaves or other shapes cut from extra dough. Set pie plate on a cookie sheet and bake at 350 degrees F for 20 to 30 minutes until crust is cooked and lightly brown.

GADO GADO

This Indonesian dish of vegetables and tofu topped with a
spicy peanut sauce makes an impressive dinner.
Serve warm or at room temperature with rice.

SERVES 6-8

3 cups peeled & cubed yam or sweet potato
2 cups cauliflower florets
1 cup julienned carrots
1 cup halved green beans

Steam vegetables over boiling water until just tender, 10 to 15 minutes. Set aside.

1 block tofu, pressed, drained & cut into 1" cubes
3 Tbsp. tamari

PREHEAT OVEN TO 375 DEGREES F. In a small bowl, gently toss tofu cubes with tamari to coat. Place on oiled baking sheet and bake until brown and crispy, 12 to 15 minutes. Set aside.

2 cups shredded Napa cabbage
½ cup chopped green onions
1 cup ¼-inch slices English cucumber

Arrange attractively with tofu and steamed vegetables on a platter. Set aside.

1 cup unsweetened coconut milk
½ cup crunchy peanut butter
1 large clove garlic, minced
¼ cup Indo Sweet Soy (see page 118)
Zest of ½ lemon
3 Tbsp. lemon juice
1 dried red chili, crumbled
½ tsp. salt
2 Tbsp. rice syrup

Mix together well in a small saucepan, and bring to a boil over medium heat. Reduce heat and simmer for 10 minutes until thickened. While still warm, pour over platter of arranged vegetables. Pass extra sauce in a pitcher for use at the table.

CONTINUED

Optional garnishes:
2 hard boiled eggs, sliced
Cherry tomatoes
Roasted peanuts, chopped

Decorate platter with garnishes, if desired.

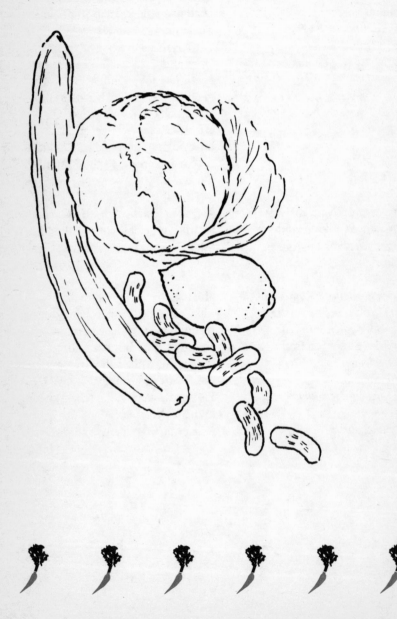

GARLIC FRIED NOODLES

For serious garlic lovers, this salad is heaven!
We suggest serving it with a mild miso soup
and a cucumber salad.

SERVES 4

6 cups spring water
8 ounces Udon Noodles

Bring water to a rapid boil in a 3-quart pot. Break noodles in half, drop into water and stir. Every time water returns to a boil add a small amount of cold water. Repeat and continue cooking until the noodles are al dente. Drain, then rinse in cold water.

2 Tbsp. sesame oil
2 whole dried hot chili pods

Heat oil and chilis in a wok over medium heat and cook for 2 minutes. Carefully remove chilis and any seeds and discard. Leave oil in wok.

6 large cloves garlic, minced fine
6 large cloves garlic, sliced in thin rounds

Add garlic to hot oil and sauté for 2 minutes. (Don't be afraid to use all this garlic — live with gusto! The garlic slices add a nice touch.)

¾ cup diced green onion, cut on diagonal
1 cup snow peas, halved on diagonal
1 (14 oz.) can baby corn, drained & left whole
¼ cup sesame seeds
Salt to taste
½ Tbsp. black pepper
¼ cup finely diced red bell pepper
3 Tbsp. toasted sesame oil
3 Tbsp. tamari

Add vegetables to garlic and continue to stir fry for 4 to 5 minutes more. When finished, place vegetables in a large bowl. Quickly stir fry cooked noodles in the same wok and add to bowl. Add the remaining ingredients and toss well. Adjust seasoning. Serve hot to bring out the garlic flavour.

OVEN ROASTED TEMPEH AND VEGETABLES

This slow-roasted stew of vegetables and tempeh in a rich brown gravy will remind you of Sunday dinners at Grandmother's house.

SERVES 4

1 (8½ oz.) square tempeh, at room
    temperature
3 Tbsp. tamari
1 Tbsp. sunflower or other light oil

PREHEAT OVEN TO 400 DEGREES F. Cut tempeh into cubes. Toss with tamari and bake on oiled cookie sheet for 12 minutes or until crisp. Remove from oven and REDUCE HEAT TO 350 DEGREES.

1 Tbsp. sunflower oil
¼ cup tamari
¼ cup white unbleached flour
¼ cup nutritional yeast (not baking
    yeast)
¼ cup tahini
2 tsp. dried basil
1 tsp. ground rosemary
2 tsp. dried marjoram
1 tsp. ground sage
½ tsp. black pepper

In the bottom of a heavy 2-quart pot, over medium heat, whisk oil, tamari, flour, yeast and tahini to form a smooth paste. Whisk in herbs and simmer for 5 minutes, stirring often.

2-3 cups spring water

Whisk in water to form a thin gravy (this will thicken on its own as it bakes) and simmer for 10 minutes. Remove from heat.

2 cups peeled & cubed potatoes
1 cup peeled & cubed carrots
½ cup peeled & cubed celeriac
¾ cup chopped celery (1" lengths)
¾ cup coarsely chopped onions

In a 3-quart Dutch oven with a lid, combine raw vegetables and gravy, stirring gently until combined. Bake, covered, for 45 minutes, stirring once or twice. Add more water if needed.

CONTINUED

¾ cup halved mushrooms
½ cup frozen peas

Add mushrooms and peas along with the cooked tempeh to the stew, stir gently and return to oven for another 15 to 20 minutes. Stir gently and serve immediately.

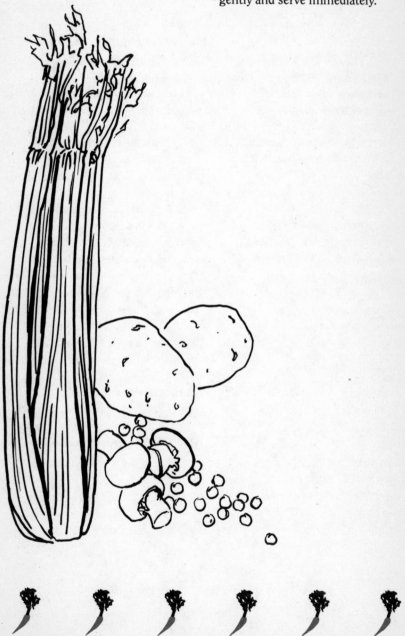

TRANSYLVANIAN MUSHROOM RAGOUT

*A rich and satisfying Romanian dish. Serve with rice,
egg noodles or as John's mother would, over polenta.*

SERVES 4

¼ cup walnut oil (or other light oil
   or butter)
2 cups finely diced onions
1 clove garlic, minced
1 Tbsp. sweet Hungarian paprika
Salt & pepper to taste

Heat oil over medium heat in a heavy-bottomed 4-quart pot with lid. Add onions and garlic and sauté for 10 minutes, stirring occasionally. Add paprika, salt and pepper and sauté 2 more minutes.

2 lbs. fresh whole mushrooms,
   cleaned & stems trimmed

Add fresh mushrooms and sauté until mushrooms begin to release their liquid — about 10 minutes.

¼ cup dry red wine
1 tsp. dried marjoram
Water or vegetable broth as needed
Flour or arrowroot, if needed

Add wine and marjoram and simmer, covered, over low heat, stirring occasionally. As liquid reduces, add water or broth a few tablespoons at a time. Simmer until onions cook down completely to a naturally thick gravy — about 45 minutes. Whisk in flour or arrowroot a tablespoon at a time if needed to thicken gravy.

½ cup chopped fresh Italian parsley

Stir in parsley and serve immediately over hot noodles, rice . or polenta. Appropriate on May 10, Romanian Independence Day.

MAPLE BAKED BEANS

These slow-baked beans have a sumptuous sweet taste that's a sure crowd pleaser. Great for picnics!

SERVES 4 GENEROUSLY, WITH LEFTOVERS.

2 cups great Northern beans, sorted
    & rinsed & soaked overnight in
6 cups spring water

Bring the beans and soaking water to a boil in a heavy oven-proof pot with a lid. Reduce heat and simmer for about an hour until beans are tender. Add more water only if needed to cover beans while cooking. Remove from heat.

3 cups thinly sliced onions
¼ cup corn oil

Sauté onions in the oil until well-browned. Add to bean pot.
HEAT OVEN TO 275 DEGREES F.

1 Tbsp. mustard powder
2 tsp. salt
2 Tbsp. molasses
⅓ cup maple syrup
2 cups seeded & sliced apples
½ cup tomato paste

Add to bean pot and stir well. Bake, covered, for 4 hours, stirring gently every half hour. Leave uncovered for last hour of cooking if needed to reduce liquid.

If not serving immediately, let cool completely before refrigerating.

TEXAS BBQ BEANS AND TEMPEH

Meanwhile, back at the ranch, tempeh rustlers
are wrangling up a pot of these authentic barbeque beans.
Serve alone or over buns like sloppy joes, with a salad.

SERVES 4

2 cups dried kidney beans, sorted,
    rinsed & soaked overnight in
6 cups spring water

Place beans and soaking water in Dutch oven with lid and bring to a boil. Reduce heat and simmer for 2 to 3 hours, until beans are tender but not falling apart. Add more water during cooking if needed. When cooked, remove from heat and drain, reserving liquid for sauce.

2 Tbsp. tamari
1 tsp. chili powder
½ tsp. dried mustard powder
¼ tsp. black pepper
1 (8½ oz.) square tempeh, thawed &
    cubed
corn oil

PREHEAT OVEN TO 400 DEGREES F. In a small bowl, mix tamari with spices. Marinate tempeh cubes in this mix for 30 minutes. Bake on oiled cookie sheets for 12 to 15 minutes until brown and crispy. Add to drained, cooked beans. REDUCE OVEN TO 350 DEGREES.

2 Tbsp. corn oil
1 cup chopped onions
2 large cloves garlic, minced
2 tsp. chili powder
4 tsp. dried mustard powder
2 tsp. dried ground sage
Cayenne pepper to taste

Heat corn oil in a skillet. Over medium-high heat, sauté onions and garlic with spices until tender.

CONTINUED

⅓ cup tomato paste
1 cup honey-sweetened catsup
5 Tbsp. molasses
2 tsp. horseradish
3 cups liquid from cooked beans
Salt to taste

1 cup chopped fresh tomatoes

Reduce heat to medium, stir wet ingredients into onions, and simmer for 20 minutes. Do not let it boil. Check for taste, correct seasonings and stir into cooked beans. Bake the beans, covered, for one hour, stirring occasionally and adding more liquid if needed.

Remove from oven and stir in chopped tomatoes. Serve hot.

TOFU CANNELONI

*These pasta roll-ups make an attractive dairy-free entrée.
They're also quick and easy to make!*

TO MAKE 12 CANNELONI

3 blocks tofu, pressed, drained &
    crumbled
1 cup diced onion
½ cup chopped parsley
1 clove garlic
¼ cup chopped fresh mint leaves (or
    4 tsp. dried mint)
Salt & pepper to taste

PREHEAT OVEN TO 300 DEGREES F.
Process together in food processor
to make a smooth paste. If mixing
by hand, mince the garlic first, then
stir all ingredients vigorously.

1 cup finely grated carrots

In a mixing bowl, stir together
carrots and blended tofu.

1 (10 oz.) pkg. fresh lasagna noodles
(or 12 pieces of fresh pasta 6" x 4")

Cut noodles to desired size. Place ⅓
to ½ cup of the tofu mix on one end
of each noodle. Roll up, making
sure ends overlap and that each
canneloni is evenly filled at both
side ends.

Place canneloni on well oiled pans,
not touching. Brush tops lightly
with oil. Cover pan with foil.
Bake for 20 minutes.

¾ cup seasoned tomato sauce

Heat sauce gently on stove. Place
canneloni on plates or serving
platter. Spoon warm sauce over
them. Garnish with parsley or basil
leaves.

SPRING ROLLS

These crispy vegetarian spring rolls have been a favourite Saturday attraction at The Big Carrot for years. They are baked, not fried, and are stuffed with assorted vegetables and tofu.

MAKES 8

1 cube tofu, pressed & drained
2 Tbsp. sesame oil
2 Tbsp. tamari

PREHEAT THE OVEN TO 425 DEGREES F. Slice the tofu into ¼-inch slices, brush on both sides with oil and tamari, and bake on a cookie sheet for 15 minutes, until puffy and brown. Remove from oven, let cool and slice again into thin strips 1-inch long.

2 Tbsp. sesame oil
2 dried hot chilis
½ tsp. dried lemon grass

Heat the oil and spices in a wok over high heat for 2 minutes. Do not let it smoke. Strain oil, discarding spices, rinse and dry wok and return flavoured oil to wok.

2 large cloves garlic, minced
1 Tbsp. grated fresh ginger
¼ cup finely diced green onion
2 tsp. toasted sesame oil
Salt to taste

Over high heat, sauté the garlic, ginger and green onions for 2 minutes, stirring often. Add toasted sesame oil and salt and heat for 1 more minute. Remove from heat and let cool.

¾ cup grated carrot
¾ cup shredded Napa cabbage
½ cup sliced mushrooms
½ cup sliced canned water chestnuts
1½ cups bean sprouts

In a very large bowl, thoroughly mix vegetables, tofu strips and contents of wok. After stirring, move mixture to a strainer set in the bowl to allow to drain for 20 minutes.

CONTINUED

8 (8" x 8") spring roll wrappers,
    thawed and separated, placed
    flat inside a barely damp towel
Sesame oil

Place a wrapper in front of you on the diagonal so that it forms a diamond shape. Pick up a handful of the vegetable mix (about ¾ cup) and gently squeeze out any liquid. Place onto the lower point of the diamond and spread evenly in a horizontal line. Lifting the lowest point of the diamond, fold it over the filling and roll once towards the centre of the wrapper. Next lift the 2 side points of the wrapper and tuck them into the centre over the filling. Continue to roll the spring roll over and over until you reach the top point. You should have a completely enclosed, tightly wrapped package.

Place the spring roll flap side down on an oiled cookie sheet. Repeat until all filling is made into spring rolls, then lightly brush tops with oil. Make sure the spring rolls are evenly spaced and not touching each other. Bake for 10 minutes, until tops are crisp. Turn over and bake for 5 minutes more, until second side is crisp. Serve immediately, with tamari, plum sauce or sweet and sour sauce for dipping.

If you get really ambitious, this spring roll recipe can be made into 32 hors d'oeuvres. Cut each wrapper in quarters to form four even squares. Roll up a small amount of filling in each. You will need to reduce the cooking time slightly. Warning: these little spring rolls are very tasty and extremely popular. You may need to make lots.

PESTO PIZZA

Pizza is a wonderful concept, unless of course you have given up cheese. Lament no more, here is a gorgeous homemade pizza with cheese-free toppings, soon to become your favorite.

SERVES 4 (10" X 15" PIZZA)

Pesto (see recipe below)
12 oz. marinated artichoke hearts, chopped
3 large tomatoes, sliced in thin rounds
1 cup zucchini, sliced into thin rounds
¼ cup pine nuts

Make the dough (see following page) and set aside to rise. Assemble all ingredients while dough for crust is rising.

PESTO TOPPING:
2 cups densely-packed fresh basil leaves, rinsed
¼ cup pine nuts
2 large cloves garlic
zest from 1 lemon
⅓ cup virgin olive oil

Process basil, pine nuts, garlic and zest in a blender or food processor until smooth. With blender running, add oil in a thin trickle to form a thick paste. Set pesto aside. When dough is ready, assemble the pizza as follows.

ASSEMBLY:
3-4 Tbsp. corn meal

PREHEAT OVEN TO 375 DEGREES F.
Sprinkle 10" x 15" baking sheet with corn meal. Place dough in centre of sheet, and press out from the centre with your hands to cover the pan with an even layer, and form a rim of dough.

Evenly spread dough with a thin layer of pesto. Artistically arrange artichoke hearts, tomato slices and zucchini evenly over the pizza. Dot with more pesto and sprinkle with pine nuts. Bake approximately 20 minutes, until dough is well-cooked and browned.

DOUGH FOR PIZZA CRUST

Make the crust first and then assemble the toppings while it rises.

ENOUGH FOR A 10" X 15 " CRUST

1 Tbsp. dry active baking yeast
1 cup warm (not hot) water

Gently combine yeast and water in a large clean dry mixing-bowl.

1 tsp. salt
2 Tbsp. rice syrup or honey
¼ cup virgin olive oil

Whisk in salt, sweetener and oil. Let sit for 10 minutes.

1 cup unbleached hard white flour
3 cups hard whole wheat flour
Extra flour for work surface

Whisk white flour into liquid. Using a sturdy wooden spoon, stir in whole wheat flour, ½ cup at a time, until dough is too stiff to stir. You will still have whole wheat flour left at this point.

Sprinkle clean dry work surface with flour. Place dough in centre, dust with flour and knead by hand for about 10 minutes. Incorporate more of the whole wheat flour while you knead, until the dough is smooth, elastic and no longer sticky (you may not have to use all the flour). Place the dough in a clean, lightly oiled bowl, cover with a clean cloth and put aside to rise in a draft-free place for about an hour. When doubled in volume, "deflate" the dough by punching it down.

SWEET AND SOUR SOYBEANS

*A tangy sauce over protein-rich beans and
colourful vegetables make this dish a favourite.*

SERVES 4

1 cup soybeans, sorted, rinsed &
    soaked in
4 cups spring water

Bring beans and soaking water to a boil in a 2-quart pot. Reduce heat and simmer for 4 to 5 hours, adding water and stirring as needed, until beans are tender — do not undercook. Remove from heat and drain. Place beans in a large bowl and set aside.

¼ cup sesame oil
1 green pepper, cut into large cubes
    or triangles
1 red pepper, cut into large cubes or
    triangles
⅓ cup chopped onions
⅓ cup chopped celery
½ cup peeled & diagonally sliced
    carrots

Heat oil in a wok. Stir fry vegetables for 3 to 4 minutes and then add to soybeans.

½ cup tamari-roasted almonds
⅓ cup frozen peas
½ cup canned pineapple tidbits, juice
    reserved

Add to cooked soybeans.

2 Tbsp. honey
1 tsp. grated fresh ginger
2 Tbsp. tamari
3 Tbsp. apple cider vinegar
½ cup reserved pineapple juice
½ Tbsp. crushed dried chilis
1 clove garlic, minced

Whisk together in a heavy-bottomed saucepan over medium heat. Allow to boil for 2 minutes. Strain liquid to remove garlic and chilis. Return liquid to pan, discarding garlic and chilis.

CONTINUED

*1 Tbsp. arrowroot powder
dissolved in 2 Tbsp. water*

Whisk arrowroot and water into sauce and continue cooking until sauce is glossy and thick. Add to soybeans and stir well. Serve hot over rice.

BAKING

There are few things better in the world than the smell of home baked goodies. It has been said that treats from the oven "give shy people the strength to go on." But baked goods can be an unwelcome temptation for those trying to avoid wheat, refined sugar or dairy products. So we've come up with recipes which offer a variety of flours and sweeteners to work with. Many use flour other than wheat, some avoid eggs, none of them use refined white sugar.

But most importantly, they are all delicious! We can say this with assurance, as we felt morally obliged to do strenuous testing and repeated quality checks — batch after batch of muffins and desserts had to be sampled — just to be sure you were getting the best, you understand. No sacrifice is too great...

ORANGE DATE MUFFINS

*These moist muffins are naturally sweetened
with dates and oranges — delicious!*

MAKES 12 MUFFINS

*2 medium seedless oranges (try to
 buy oranges with unblemished
 skins)*

PREHEAT OVEN TO 350 DEGREES F.
Bring a 2-quart pot half
full of water to a boil.
Place whole oranges into water and
boil for 5 minutes. Remove and let
cool enough to handle. This step is
to remove bitterness from the skins.
Chop oranges coarsely, removing
any blemishes on peel.
Place in a food processor and
process until mushy but with some
small bits of peel left.
Remove to large mixing bowl.

2 cups chopped, pitted dates
1½ cups orange juice

Put dates and half the orange juice
in the processor. Start and quickly
stop the processor a few times, then
process steadily until dates are
reduced to small pieces. Add to
oranges, along with the rest of the
orange juice.

3 medium eggs
½ cup soya margarine

Use processor to cream eggs and
margarine, then add to the orange
mixture. Combine well.

CONTINUED

3 cups whole wheat flour
2 tsp. baking powder
1 tsp. salt

Mix dry ingredients in separate bowl, then add to wet mixture, stirring until just mixed. Batter will be fairly stiff.

Line muffin cups with paper liners or grease well. Fill cups with mixture. Bake for 20 to 25 minutes. Muffins will be golden brown with slightly crunchy edges. These are dense muffins, so do not underbake. If you do, the centres will be doughy.

SUNRISE MUFFINS

*Our baker concocted the recipe for this muffin -
a healthy breakfast treat crammed with delicious goodies.*

MAKES 12 LARGE MUFFINS

4 eggs

PREHEAT OVEN TO 350 DEGREES F.
Beat eggs well with whisk in a large
mixing bowl.

⅔ cup sunflower oil
1½ cups apple cider or juice
1 cup grated carrots
½ cup raisins

Add to beaten eggs and mix together
thoroughly.

2 cups unbleached white flour
1 cup whole wheat flour
½ cup shredded coconut
½ cup chopped raw almonds
2½ tsp. cinnamon
2½ tsp. baking powder

Mix well in a separate bowl.
Add to wet mixture, combining just
until dry mixture is absorbed. Grease
muffin tins generously, or line with
paper muffin cups. Divide the batter
equally amongst the cups. They will
be heaped higher than the rim.

Bake for 20 to 25 minutes. The
muffins should be toasty brown on
top.

BANANA BRAN MUFFINS

These moist and flavourful muffins are easy to make.

MAKES 12

1½ cups unbleached white flour
½ cup whole wheat flour
5 tsp. baking powder
1½ cups bran
½ cup wheat germ
½ Tbsp. cinnamon
1 tsp. salt

PREHEAT OVEN TO 350 DEGREES F.
Combine dry ingredients in a bowl.

4 eggs
⅔ cup sunflower or light vegetable
    oil
2 cups mashed bananas (approx. 5
    medium bananas)
½ cup honey

In a separate bowl, beat eggs. Add
other wet ingredients and mix
thoroughly. Combine with dry
ingredients, stirring until just
moistened. Line muffin tins with
paper muffin cups, or grease well.
Spoon batter into prepared muffin
tins. Bake for 20 minutes. Remove
from pans and let cool.

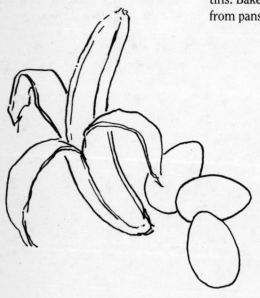

SANTE FE MAPLE PIÑON MUFFINS

*Cornmeal and toasted piñon (pine nuts) capture
the taste of a New Mexico morning, in these
wheat-free, dairy-free muffins.*

MAKES 18 MUFFINS

1¼ cup corn flour
1 cup cornmeal
1 tsp. cinnamon
4 tsp. baking powder
½ tsp. salt
1 cup toasted & ground pine nuts

PREHEAT OVEN TO 400 DEGREES F.
Mix dry ingredients in a bowl.

2 large eggs
1 tsp. vanilla
⅔ cup maple syrup
½ cup (scant) corn oil
1¼ cups soymilk

In a second bowl, lightly beat eggs.
Whisk in vanilla, maple syrup, oil
and soymilk until blended.
Combine wet and dry ingredients.
Stir until just mixed. Batter will be
very wet. Pour or ladle into oiled or
paper lined muffin tins, filling cups
¾ full. Bake for 20 minutes until
golden brown. These muffins will
not rise very much.

*To toast the piñons, or pine nuts, place on a cookie sheet
in a 400 degree F oven for 5 to 10 minutes. Watch closely
and stir occasionally, until evenly brown and toasted.
Process briefly in a food processor or grind to a
powder with a mortar and pestle. Make extra and store
in the freezer.*

CAROB COCONUT MUFFINS

*These dark, moist muffins are almost
like cupcakes — enjoy them!*

MAKES 12 MUFFINS

¾ cup toasted & chopped walnuts
3¼ cups whole wheat flour
¾ cup carob powder
1 tsp. salt
1½ tsp. baking powder
¾ cup shredded coconut

PREHEAT OVEN TO 350 DEGREES F.
Combine dry ingredients in a large
mixing bowl.

1¾ cups apple cider
⅓ cup tahini
⅓ cup rice syrup
¾ cup maple syrup
1 tsp. vanilla

Combine wet ingredients in a
separate bowl, stirring well with a
fork or whisk. Add wet ingredients
to dry, stirring until just mixed.
Grease muffin cups or line with
paper liners, then fill with batter.
Bake for 10 minutes, rotate pan for
even baking and bake for another 10
minutes. Remove from pan and let
cool.

RICE PUDDINGS

*These glazed puddings make pretty individual desserts
served warm, but act like muffins when they have cooled.
An old family favourite in a new format.*

2 cups short grain brown rice
6 cups (scant) spring water
2 tsp. salt
1" cinnamon stick
1 cup wild rice

In a 3-quart pot with a lid, bring water to a boil. Add brown rice, salt and cinnamon stick, bring back to a boil, then reduce heat to a simmer. Simmer for about 45 minutes until all the water is absorbed and rice is tender, adding wild rice to the pot for the last 20 minutes of cooking. Remove from heat, discard cinnamon stick and spread rice out in a shallow tray or pan to cool completely.

¼ cup unsalted butter
3 Tbsp. rice syrup
1 Tbsp. vanilla extract
½ tsp. salt
1 Tbsp. cinnamon
⅓ tsp. cloves

Melt together in a small heavy saucepan over low heat, stirring to combine. Pour over cooked rice, stir to combine and let cool completely. PREHEAT OVEN TO 350 DEGREES F.

5 large eggs
1 cup currants

In a large bowl, beat the eggs, then add the currants. Add the cooled rice and butter mixture. Combine thoroughly. Grease muffin tins generously, or line with paper liners. Pack the rice mixture into the cups to form tightly compressed and rounded mounds. Bake for approximately 30 minutes until

CONTINUED

golden brown and firm. Note that some of the egg may have cooked out and spread over the top of the muffin pans; do not panic, just wash pans extra well when finished. Remove muffins carefully from pans and let cool on a rack lined with wax paper or foil.

3 Tbsp. rice syrup
2 Tbsp. water
¼ tsp. cinnamon
2-3 Tbsp. toasted almond slices
    (optional)

In small saucepan used above, gently heat rice syrup and water with cinnamon to form a glaze, spooning a bit over the top of each muffin while still warm.

If desired, sprinkle almonds on top of muffins for decoration.

CARROT ZUCCHINI BREAD

You'd never guess that zucchini could taste as good as it does in this quick bread made with durum wheat. Serve it for breakfast or make an almond butter sandwich for lunch.

MAKES TWO 4" X 8" LOAVES

2½ cups roasted durum flour
1 Tbsp. baking powder
1 tsp. baking soda
1 tsp. cinnamon
1 tsp. salt

PREHEAT OVEN TO 325 DEGREES F.
Mix dry ingredients in a large mixing bowl.

2 eggs, beaten
⅔ cup sunflower oil
⅔ cup honey
1⅓ cups grated zucchini
1⅓ cups peeled & grated carrots

In a separate bowl, combine wet ingredients until well mixed. Stir in zucchini and carrots. Add to dry ingredients, mixing thoroughly. Batter will be stiff.

Lightly oil two loaf pans. Divide the batter in half and press firmly into pans. Bake for 30 minutes or until a knife or toothpick inserted in the centre comes out clean.

Roasting certain flours like durum or oat improves the flavour of the finished product by removing the bitter taste of the raw flour. To roast flour, bake on a rimmed cookie sheet for 20 minutes at 325 degrees F, stirring once. Let cool before using or storing in an airtight container.

CRANBERRY ORANGE BREAD

This colourful quick bread is perfect for brunches or tea time. It combines the tartness of cranberries and the sweetness of honey, with a hint of orange.

MAKES TWO 4" X 8" LOAVES

2⅔ cups roasted durum flour
    (see page 97)
2 tsp. baking powder
1 tsp. baking soda
1 tsp. salt

PREHEAT OVEN TO 325 DEGREES F. Mix dry ingredients in a large mixing bowl.

2 eggs, beaten
3 Tbsp. safflower oil
⅔ cup honey
1 cup orange juice

In a second bowl, whisk wet ingredients until thoroughly mixed. (A whisk will have better results than a spoon.)

1½ cups chopped cranberries
⅔ cup chopped walnuts

Add wet to dry ingredients, mixing thoroughly. Stir in cranberries and walnuts. Batter will be stiff.

Lightly oil two loaf pans. Divide the batter in half and press firmly into pans. Bake for 30 minutes, or until a knife or toothpick inserted in the centre comes out clean.

QUICK DAIRY-FREE PIE CRUST

A simple, dairy-free pastry that is easy to work with.

MAKES 2 CRUSTS FOR 9" PIE PLATE

1 cup whole wheat pastry (soft) flour
1 cup unbleached white flour
⅓ (scant) cup corn oil or other light oil
1 tsp. salt
Zest of 1 orange, or pinch of mace or ground coriander (optional)
½ cup ice-cold spring water

Lightly mix ingredients with a fork or your hands. Mix only until dough holds together and is the consistency of your ear lobe. Dough should be slightly "wet" rather than dry. You may have leftover flour that is not incorporated.

Now wipe the flour off your ear lobe, and wrap the dough tightly in plastic wrap. Refrigerate dough for 30 minutes to make handling easier. Knead gently 8 to 10 times on lightly floured board and roll out as desired.

APPLE STRUDEL WITH LEMON AND WALNUTS

A delicious Old World dessert, impressive enough for company, but simple to make.

5 large apples (Granny Smith preferable)
¾ cup toasted walnut pieces
Zest of 1 lemon

Peel and core apples and process through fine slice disc of food processor. If working by hand, slice on the thin-slice section of a hand-held grater and stop before reaching core.
OR peel, core and quarter the apples and slice crosswise as thinly as possible.
Add walnuts and zest to apples.

3 Tbsp. rice syrup or honey
3 Tbsp. lemon juice
2 Tbsp. flour
Spring water (if needed)

Mix rice syrup, lemon juice and flour together to form a smooth paste, adding water if needed. Stir into apples.

16 oz. pkg. frozen filo pastry, thawed
⅓ – ½ cup walnut oil

PREHEAT OVEN TO 375 DEGREES F.
Lightly oil a large rimless baking sheet. Place one sheet of filo on oiled pan and lightly brush with oil. Repeat until you have a stack of 6 sheets of filo. Mound apple filling in a rough circle approximately 2 inches thick in the centre of the filo.

Trim the filo layers into a rough circle with a sharp knife or scissors, leaving a 2 to 3 inch border of filo around the apple mixture. Cover

CONTINUED

apple mixture with 6 more sheets of oiled filo. Trim to fit bottom circle of filo.

Seal the edges of the strudel together to form a crust, by rolling up the extra two inches of filo. Gently lifting the top and bottom layers together, tightly roll the outside edge of the circle of filo in toward the apple mixture, all the way around the pie. Lightly brush the top of the strudel and the rolled crust with oil.

Cut steam vents into the top and bake for 20 to 25 minutes, until filo is well browned and crispy. After baking, the strudel can be decorated with walnut halves, lemon zest, fresh apple slices, etc.

PAULA'S CAROB RIPPLE TOFU "CHEESECAKE"

*A luscious glazed dessert swirled with carob —
a texture like cheesecake, but not nearly so sinful.*

SERVES 8-10

CRUST:
1½ cups graham cracker crumbs
2 Tbsp. rice syrup
¼ cup corn oil

Mix crust ingredients with a fork or pastry blender; press into bottom only of 9½" springform pan.

FILLING:
4 blocks tofu, pressed & drained
½ tsp. salt
¼ cup lemon juice
½ cup sunflower oil
½ cup rice syrup
2 tsp. vanilla
1 Tbsp. arrowroot dissolved in 2
    Tbsp. water

Process in food processor until very smooth. Set aside one cup of batter to make carob ripple. Pour half of remaining batter on top of crust. Set aside other half. PREHEAT OVEN TO 350 DEGREES F.

RIPPLE:
¼ cup carob powder

In a small bowl, mix carob powder with the one cup of reserved batter until well blended. Spoon onto batter in spring-form pan, top with remaining half of plain batter and swirl with a knife or spoon handle. Bake for 30 minutes, or until it appears set.

GLAZE:
¼ cup soymilk powder
¼ cup carob powder
½ cup water
3 Tbsp. maple syrup

Combine and bring to a boil in a small saucepan. Simmer for 10 minutes until thick.

CONTINUED

1 tsp. vanilla

Add to glaze and stir well. Working quickly, apply glaze to top of still warm cake — do not let either glaze or cake cool or both will be difficult to work with.

Toasted coconut or
Toasted almond slivers

Decorate glazed cake with coconut or nuts.

OLD-FASHIONED OATMEAL OAT BRAN COOKIES

A nostagically wonderful cookie

MAKES 24 TWO-INCH COOKIES

2 cups small flake oats
⅔ cup oat bran

PREHEAT OVEN TO 350 DEGREES F.
Combine oats and bran and toast for 5 minutes on cookie sheet. Let cool.

1⅓ cups whole wheat flour
1 Tbsp. pumpkin pie spice (a blend of cinnamon, ginger, cloves & nutmeg)
½ tsp. baking soda
½ tsp. salt

Combine dry ingredients in a mixing bowl. Set aside.

1 cup margarine, softened
1 cup Sucanat "sugar"
1 tsp. vanilla

Whip together until creamy.

2 large eggs

Add to wet ingredients and whip.

1 cup Thompson raisins

Add wet ingredients to dry and mix well. Add toasted oats, oat bran and raisins, mixing well. Drop by spoonfuls on greased baking sheet. Bake for 5 minutes, rotate pans, then bake for 5 minutes more. Remove from baking sheet and let cool.

YOUR BASIC GRANOLA

The smell of baking granola will soothe any savage beasts you have hanging around on a rainy afternoon; and creating granola additions can become an artform involving the whole family.

MAKES 16 CUPS

16 cups large flake oats
½ cup soy flour
1 cup sunflower seed oil
1 cup liquid honey

For suggested additions to the basic granola, see page 106.

PREHEAT OVEN TO 350 DEGREES F.
Pour oats into a large roasting pan with high sides. Use your hands to mix in soy flour thoroughly so that it coats each flake. Pour in oil and honey, continue to work in with hands vigorously until completely mixed.

Bake granola for 15 minutes. Remove from oven to stir thoroughly. The granola bakes faster along edges and corners, so be sure to scrape and stir these areas with a vengeance. If oats are browning too quickly, reduce heat to 300 degrees.

Return granola to the oven for 15 minutes more, remove and stir completely. Repeat for a third 15 minute session, adding any optional nuts or seeds. Check to see if granola is a consistent golden brown colour. If not, return to oven for 5 to 10 more minutes. Remove from oven.

Let cool in pan on a cooling rack so that air can circulate underneath. Stir occasionally while cooling. When cool, break up any large clumps and stir in desired additions. Store in an airtight container.

EVERYTHING BUT THE KITCHEN SINK GRANOLA

Let your imagination go and create your own favourite
combination for breakfasts or snacks.

2 Tbsp. cinnamon OR
1 Tbsp. vanilla extract

To 16 cups granola, (see page 105) add during initial mixing, before baking.

OR
2 cups chopped or slivered
almonds OR
2 cups walnut pieces OR
2 cups sesame seeds OR
2 cups sunflower seeds OR
2 cups pecan pieces

Add to 16 cups granola base during last 15 minutes of baking.

OR
2 cups raisins OR
2 cups dried blueberries OR
2 cups diced dried peaches OR
2 cups dried strawberries OR
2 cups dried apple slices OR
2 cups dried banana chips OR
2 cups pitted & chopped dates OR
2 cups carob chips

Add to 16 cups granola base, after baked and cooled. (Note: Do NOT add raisins or other dried fruits during baking.) Combine any of the ingredients listed on this page to make a new granola "recipe" (examples: "Apple Pie Granola" — dried apples and cinnamon. "Summertime" granola — dried blueberries, peaches and strawberries, etc.). You may need to play with amounts to get the right proportion of ingredients.

NOTE: if you reduce or multiply this recipe,
baking times may change. Keep a careful eye on
the granola so that it doesn't burn.

MAPLE WALNUT GRANOLA

*The rich taste of real maple syrup makes this relatively simple granola mix an extra special one and our personal favourite.
Great as a topping for a fruit cobbler.*

MAKES 12 CUPS

8 cups large flake oats
1 cup oat bran
¾ cup soy flour
½ tsp. salt
1½ tsp. cinnamon

PREHEAT OVEN TO 325 DEGREES F.
Combine dry ingredients in a large roasting pan with high sides. Use your hands to mix in bran and flour thoroughly so that each flake is coated.

1 cup canola or other light oil
1½ cups maple syrup
1 Tbsp. vanilla extract

Mix wet ingredients together, add to dry and continue to work in with hands vigorously and thoroughly until completely mixed.

Bake granola for 30 minutes, stirring thoroughly after 15 minutes. Note that granola bakes faster along edges and corners, so be sure to scrape and stir these areas well. If oats brown too quickly, reduce heat to 300 degrees.

3 cups chopped walnuts
1½ cups slivered almonds

Add nuts, stir well. Return granola to the oven for 15 minutes more, then remove and stir completely. Check to see if granola is a consistent golden brown colour; if not, return to oven for 5 to 10 more minutes, then remove from oven.

Let cool in pan on a cooling rack so that air can circulate underneath. Stir occasionally while cooling. When cool, break up any large clumps. Store in airtight container.

KAR-IN'S CRISPY RICE SQUARES

A childhood favourite revisited that's an
easy no-bake treat. Makes an 8"x 8" pan.

SERVES 6 GENEROUSLY, 3 GLUTTONOUSLY OR 1 FATALLY

¼ cup almond butter
¼ cup tahini
½ cup rice syrup

In a heavy saucepan over low heat, combine almond butter, tahini and rice syrup until softened. Remove from heat.

1 tsp. vanilla extract
¼ tsp. salt (optional)

Add and stir well.

2 cups crispy brown rice cereal
⅓ cup chopped roasted almonds
  (optional)
⅓ cup carob or chocolate chips
  (optional)
⅓ cup coconut (optional)

Fold in cereal and optional ingredients, stirring until well mixed. Press into a lightly oiled 8" x 8" pan. Chill in refrigerator for 1 to 2 hours. Slice and serve.

AND EVERYTHING ELSE...

The following is a hodgepodge of useful tidbits. Several of the recipes will stun and impress your friends when used as party dips and spreads, but also do double service as sandwich fillings to help you get through one more day of brown-bagging it.

HUMMUS

There are as many variations on this classic Mediterranean dish as there are olives on a tree. Here is our favourite — use it as a dip for vegetables or make a pita sandwich with hummus and lots of sprouts, cucumbers and tomato slices.

MAKES 4 CUPS

3 cups cooked chick peas
¾ cup liquid from chick peas or
  spring water
1 tsp. salt
4 large cloves garlic

Use canned chick peas or cook as directed below — they should be very well done for this recipe. Process with liquid, salt and garlic in a blender or food processor for 7 to 10 minutes until smooth, scraping down sides of processor once or twice with a rubber spatula.

¼ cup tahini
⅓ cup lemon juice
¼ cup olive oil

Add and process for 3 to 5 more minutes. Hummus should be somewhat thin and smooth, about the consistency of pancake batter, as it thickens when chilled.

FOR 3 CUPS COOKED CHICK PEAS (GARBANZOS):
Sort, rinse and soak 1½ cups dried chick peas overnight in 3 cups spring water. In a heavy-bottomed 2-quart pot, bring chick peas and soaking water to a boil. Reduce heat and simmer for 4 to 5 hours, stirring occasionally and adding more water as needed. When peas are tender, remove from heat and drain, reserving liquid.

BABA GANOUJ

This tangy Middle Eastern spread weds
the flavours of roasted eggplant and garlic.
Use it as a dip for raw vegetables.

MAKES 3 CUPS

2½ lbs. eggplant

PREHEAT OVEN TO 450 DEGREES F.
Pierce eggplants with a fork (very important — otherwise they "explode" in the oven...) and place on oiled baking sheet with a rim. Roast eggplants for 45 to 50 minutes until they are very tender. Remove from oven, cut off stem end and let cool. Slit eggplants open lengthwise, scrape out flesh to make 2 cups and discard skins. Place roasted eggplant in colander or strainer over a bowl to drain. This liquid is bitter and should be discarded.

¼ cup tahini
¼ cup virgin olive oil
¼ cup lemon juice
2 large cloves garlic
1 tsp. salt
½ tsp. black pepper
¼ cup chopped parsley

Combine with 2 cups of roasted eggplant pulp in a food processor or blender. Process until thoroughly combined and of even consistency. Store covered and refrigerated. Serve at room temperature.

GUACAMOLE

Welcome to Tex-Mex heaven with this authentic recipe for the incomparable avocado. Use it as a dip for tortilla chips or make a guacamole salad on a bed of shredded lettuce and tomato wedges.

SERVES 4

2 medium avocados, firm but ripe
¾ cup sour cream or unflavoured
    yogurt
Salt & pepper to taste
1 tsp. ground cumin
1-3 Tbsp. picante sauce to taste
Fresh minced cilantro to taste
    (optional)
Worcestershire sauce to taste
    (optional)
1 Tbsp. Tequila (optional)

Peel avocado, discarding peel and pit. Cut into chunks into a food processor and blend with sour cream and seasonings until smooth and creamy. If working by hand, mash with a fork, stirring vigorously until smooth.

½ cup finely diced onion
½ cup finely diced tomato
1 clove garlic, minced

Add to avocado purée in a bowl and stir with a fork until well blended.

2 Tbsp. fresh lime juice

If serving immediately, stir in lime juice. Avocado darkens in colour upon contact with air. To avoid this if not serving immediately, pour lime juice over the top, cover the bowl tightly with plastic wrap and refrigerate. Stir in the lime juice just before serving.

If you don't use dairy, substitute one block of tofu, pressed, drained, crumbled and well blended into the avocado purée to replace sour cream.

HERBED CHEESE SPREAD

A tasty sandwich spread that is easy to make.

3 cups packed, finely grated medium
    cheddar cheese
⅔ cup unflavoured yogurt
1 Tbsp. Dijon mustard
½ cup diced green onion
2 cloves garlic, minced
½ cup chopped fresh parsley
3 Tbsp. minced fresh tarragon
(or 3 tsp. dried)
2 Tbsp. minced fresh marjoram (or 2
    tsp. dried)
Salt & black pepper to taste
2-3 drops Tabasco sauce

Mix all ingredients until thoroughly
blended. Store tightly sealed in the
refrigerator.

You can create variations of this spread by making it with Jarlsberg and fresh dill or Monterey Jack, chili powder, and canned green chilis, etc.

DEVILLED TOFU SPREAD

*This colourful sandwich spread is similar to egg salad
but made with high-protein, low-fat tofu.*

MAKES 4 CUPS

3 blocks tofu, pressed & drained
½ cup eggless mayonnaise
3 cloves garlic, minced
1 Tbsp. rice syrup or honey
Salt & pepper to taste
½ Tbsp. turmeric
3 drops Tabasco sauce
1½ Tbsp. mild Dijon mustard
2 Tbsp. lemon juice

Crumble tofu into a food processor
and process with mayonnaise and
seasonings until smooth and thick.
Stop and scrape down the sides of
the processor several times with a
rubber spatula. If working by hand,
mash and stir vigorously to form a
smooth paste.

½ cup finely diced green onion
½ cup finely diced red bell pepper
½ cup finely diced green bell pepper
¼ cup finely diced fresh parsley

Combine with the tofu spread in a
bowl and stir well until thoroughly
blended.

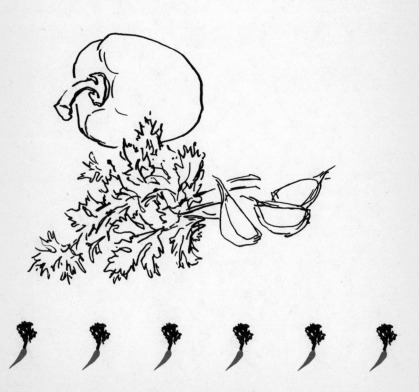

115

PICO DE GALLO

*This "salsa fresca" is a favourite condiment — fresh crunchy
vegetables with a bit of fire and the predominant flavour of cilantro.
Eaten with tortilla chips, it can be addictive.*

MAKES 4 CUPS

2 cups finely diced fresh ripe
    tomatoes
1 cup finely diced onion
2 cloves garlic, minced
1 cup finely diced green bell pepper
1-2 fresh jalapeño or other hot
    pepper, seeded & minced
½ cup minced fresh cilantro
¼ cup fresh lime juice
Salt & pepper to taste

Combine all ingredients in a bowl,
tossing gently with a fork until well
mixed. Serve chilled, spooned over
tacos or scooped up with corn
tortilla chips.

TOFUNAISE

This smooth and creamy blend makes a great sandwich spread or salad dressing — like mayonnaise without the eggs.

MAKES 3 CUPS

2 blocks tofu, pressed & drained
¼ cup lemon juice
2 tsp. Dijon mustard
1 tsp. salt
1 tsp. honey

Crumble tofu into blender or food processor. Blend with lemon, mustard, salt and honey until smooth. Scrape down sides with a rubber spatula.

1 cup sunflower or soy oil

With blender running, trickle in oil in slow stream, and blend for one minute.
Store refrigerated in clean, airtight container for up to one week.

INDONESIAN SWEET SOY

*Primarily used in making gado gado, this
excellent marinade and seasoning keeps indefinitely.
Use it to baste tofu before baking.*

MAKES 1½-2 CUPS

¾ cup Sucanat "sugar"

Heat Sucanat in a heavy-bottomed saucepan over medium heat, stirring often until it begins to melt and caramelize.

1¼ cups tamari
2 cloves garlic, crushed
2 large star anise pods
1 piece dried tangerine peel
1 Tbsp. Szechuan peppercorns
¼ cup spring water

Add to Sucanat and simmer until sauce is slightly thickened and Sucanat is completely dissolved — about 15 minutes. Let cool, then pour into a clean glass jar with a tight-fitting lid — do not strain. Cover and refrigerate. Keeps for up to 2 years.

The somewhat exotic ingredients for this recipe can be found at your natural foods market or at an East Indian or Chinese market. The end result makes the time spent searching well worthwhile.

EGGPLANT PATE

A beautiful orange colour and the distinctive tang of roasted eggplant make this an unusual and appealing party spread.

MAKES ONE 4" X 8" LOAF

2 cups roasted eggplant pulp
   (see below)
1 cup tahini
⅓ cup barley or other flour
3 eggs
3 cloves garlic
2 tsp. salt
1 tsp. black pepper
½ tsp. ground rosemary
2 tsp. honey
½ cup tomato paste

PREHEAT OVEN TO 300 DEGREES F.
Process all ingredients together in a food processor to make a smooth paste. Grease loaf pan, line with wax paper and grease again. Fill with eggplant mixture and cover tightly with foil. Place loaf pan in a casserole dish that is an inch or two larger all around. Fill casserole dish with water to a depth of one to two inches. This creates a water bath. Place the loaf pan in its water bath in the oven and bake for 50 minutes. Uncover the paté and bake for 10 minutes more until a knife inserted in the middle comes out clean. Let cool on a cooling rack for 10 minutes. Invert pan onto serving plate and unmold. Remove and discard wax paper. Let cool completely. Garnish with parsley. This paté freezes well for up to a month when tightly wrapped.

CONTINUED

TO ROAST EGGPLANT:

PREHEAT OVEN TO 450 DEGREES F. Rinse 2½ lbs. eggplant. Pierce eggplants with a fork (very important — otherwise they "explode" in the oven...) and place on oiled baking sheet with a rim. Roast eggplants for 45 to 50 minutes until they are very tender. Remove from oven, cut off stem end and let cool. Slit eggplants open lengthwise, scrape out flesh to make 2 cups and discard skins. Place roasted eggplant in colander or strainer over a bowl to drain. This liquid is bitter and should be discarded.

A GUIDE TO INGREDIENTS

You may already be familiar and comfortable with many of the ingredients used in this book. If, however, you are not sure if miso is vegetable or mineral, then a world of new tastes awaits you. This glossary can act as a field guide to the characters and habitats of the herbs, vegetables and grains that are found in our recipes. Many of these are only just now migrating to North American tables and cupboards after distinguished centuries as the mainstays of other, older cuisines.

Reading through this glossary will leave you less bewildered in the exotic produce section of your local market, as you will be on a first-name basis with jicama, cilantro, burdock and other global bon vivants. You will learn the ins and outs of agar agar and how to tame tofu. Using this book may even enhance your social standing, as you will be able to 'name drop' with the best of them; the secrets of quinoa, gado gado and gazpacho will all be yours to work into dinner party conversations.

But seriously, folks, that's not the original intention of this glossary or of these recipes. What we hope to do is to introduce you to a world of delicious ingredients, to expand your repertoire of dishes that are as appealing to the eye and taste bud as they are healthy to eat. If you are wanting or needing to change your diet to include more whole grains, less refined sugars, more fresh vegetables, and if possibly the whole idea intimidates you a little, then have courage and read on...

A GLOSSARY OF TERMS

AGAR AGAR — a thickening agent made from a sea vegetable, it comes in flakes or in clear bars. Dissolve in hot water or broth, or sprinkle into sauces or dressings while whisking or blending to thicken.

ARAME — a sea vegetable naturally high in minerals. Rinse this dark, dried algae well, boil for a few minutes, let soak 3 to 4 hours and then drain. Use in salads or in soup. Store dried in a cool dry place; cooked, it keeps tightly covered in the fridge for 4 to 5 days.

ARROWROOT — an easy substitute for cornstarch, arrowroot flour is the bland, thickening starch from a tuber similar to the cassava plant. Mix with a little water or cooking liquid to make a smooth paste before adding it to hot liquids. Stir the paste gradually into soup or sauce — do not overcook once thickened.

BURDOCK — this Japanese root vegetable is long, thin and pale brown on the outside, with a white interior and pleasant taste. To use, lightly scrub the exterior clean; no need to peel it. We suggest choosing roots that are no bigger than 1" in diameter, slicing them in very thin diagonals, and then stir frying them for use in vegetable stir frys or soups. It can also be grated. Burdock is believed to act as a blood purifier.

CAROB — sometimes known as a substitute for chocolate, though carob fans insist that it stands on its own. Sold as a powder like cocoa or in chips, carob is caffeine-free, relatively high in calcium and low in fat. Use the powdered form as you would cocoa, for baking or in a warm beverage.

CAYENNE — a red spice ground from very hot red peppers, it should be added sparingly, a few grains at a time.

CELERIAC — Don't let the gnarled, sometimes muddy appearance of this root vegetable fool you. A member of the celery family, it has a hint of celery taste, and acts beautifully as a base for cream-style soups. Grated raw as a salad base or cubed and boiled in stews, it should be peeled and cleaned completely before use.

CHILIS — or peppers as they are more commonly called, add interest to life — they range from mild and sweet to ones so fiery they can provide tonsillectomies without benefit of surgery. You can't always tell from the outside how hot any individual pepper will be, so proceed with caution and a sense of adventure.

Peppers come fresh, dried or canned. Mild peppers are generally called bell peppers — they come in red, yellow, and most commonly, green. The green ones are sometimes called sweet peppers, poblanos or Anaheims, while the long thin yellow ones are called banana peppers. All three colours can be used interchangeably, though the red and yellow are wonderful for adding visual accents to dishes. To use, remove seeds, stems, veins (the membrane inside the pepper that attaches the seeds to the flesh), and any blemishes; then chop, dice, julienne or cut into thin rings.

Hot fresh chilis are usually smaller, from the size of your thumb (jalapeños) on down to small green serranos or the tiny curving red firebombs that are picturesquely known as "Devil's toenails." Equally hot are the beautiful red, yellow and pale green peppers shaped like Chinese lanterns, called "Scotch bonnets" or Jamaican peppers. When selecting hot peppers, pick out firm, plump, unblemished ones. Handle with great caution — carefully remove and discard the stem, veins and seeds (the hottest part!). Mince very fine, then add it raw or cooked to soups, stir frys and dressings. Thoroughly wash your knife, cutting board and hands. When you handle fresh or dried hot peppers, do not touch your face — eyes especially! — without washing your hands first. Extreme discomfort and the feeling that your skin is on fire can result if you rub your eyes or lips after cutting peppers.

Dried chilis are usually red and hot — you can buy them whole, crumbled or powdered. To use whole dried chilis in dressings, soak 1 to 2 chilis in a few tablespoons of hot water for 5 minutes. After soaking, mince or put through the blender, adding the water from soaking to the dressing. To cook beans, simply drop one or two peppers in the pot when the beans start to cook. When beans are tender, remove and discard chili pods.

To flavour cooking oil, heat oil and chili pod(s) over medium-high heat for 3 to 5 minutes to allow oil to pick up the heat of the chili — remove and discard pod and any seeds, then use flavoured oil to sauté vegetables with added zest.

Canned chilis are available pickled or roasted, and range from mild to hot. Eat the pickled ones as condiments; for roasted chilis, dice and add to beans, or bake into corn bread for a distinctive Southwestern taste.

CHILI POWDER — this dried and powdered form of a hot red pepper comes in a variety of strengths and sometimes has other spices and seasonings added to it (notably sugar and salt in commercial mixes). Add it a tablespoon at a time while sautéeing vegetables or simmering beans to achieve desired flavour and heat — allowing chili powder to cook in with other ingredients can prevent a raw, bitter edge that it sometimes has when uncooked.

CILANTRO — a pretty herb that looks remarkably similar to flat leaf parsley, but can be distinguished by the pungent, slightly sweet aroma it imparts when you crush a leaf. It is used widely around the world, appearing in Chinese, Mexican and Indian kitchens among others. The leaf portion of the coriander plant, it is sometimes referred to as Chinese parsley. Its distinctive taste tends to either be loved or hated, but if you develop a taste for it, you will find that you are adding it to rice, hot sauces and relishes, salad dressings, and soups. Combines well with garlic and lemon or lime juice.

CORIANDER — the seeds of the coriander plant (the leaf portion is usually referred to as cilantro), ground to a powder and used in both Mexican and Indian cooking. Combines well with cumin, mustard seeds, anise and fennel.

DAHL — a simple Indian dish of yellow split peas or lentils cooked with curry spices.

DAIKON RADISH — a large white radish with a bit of a bite eaten raw but a slightly sweet taste when cooked. Peel fresh daikon and grate it for salads, or dice or julienne it to cook in stir frys or soups. Dried shredded daikon is available in packages, and can be rehydrated by boiling for 20 to 30 minutes and then being left to soak for 2 to 3 hours. Drain and use as fresh.

DULSE — a sea vegetable found in the North Atlantic with broad reddish purple leaves. It has a mild salty taste. Dried dulse can be toasted in the oven and then crumbled and sprinkled on vegetables or rice.

FILO — a paper-thin wheat pastry, used to make desserts and savoury dishes that are light and flaky. Filo is either layered flat with different fillings, or used as a "wrapper" for sweet or savoury fillings to make large or individual "packages." It is usually available in the freezer section of grocery stores and, while intimidating at first, is really quite easy to work with.

GINGER — the pungent bite of fresh ginger mellows slightly with cooking to add an essential taste to Oriental cuisine. Store the fresh root in an airtight container; do not refrigerate. To use, peel away the tough brown peel and grate with a fine grater or slice into thin slices and then mince. Fresh ginger root is much preferable to the dried powder form, but if it is unavailable, then substitute ⅛ teaspoon dried for each tablespoon of fresh ginger required. Use it in salad dressings, soups and stir frys.

HERBS — dried or fresh, herbs are an essential part of good cooking. The word herb refers to the leaves and stems of various flavourful plants such as basil, oregano, parsley, dill, etc., which are used to impart delicate or pungent tastes to raw and cooked dishes. Learning to cook with fresh herbs is a delicious adventure; experiment to find new combinations that please you. Dried herbs have more concentrated flavour, so when using fresh, add three times the amount called for in dried form. Keep fresh herbs in the refrigerator. Store dried herbs in airtight containers in a cool spot out of direct sun. Purchase them in small amounts and replace them often, so that they don't lose their flavour.

HIZIKI — similar to arame, used in the same way, although with a slightly stronger taste and thicker strands. You may want to break up the dried algae into shorter, more manageable pieces before cooking, as they swell and expand greatly.

HONEY — a sweetener produced by bees, honey takes its distinctive flavour from whatever flowers the bees drew nectar. Buckwheat honey is stronger tasting, while clover and orange blossom are milder. Try several to find your own favourite. Honey is more intensely sweet than white sugar, so reduce the amount used when substituting by about half. Using honey instead of white sugar will also somewhat affect the texture of baked goods.

JICAMA — This delicious and versatile root vegetable comes from Mexico. If you peel away the pale brown leathery skin, you will find a crisp, moist, slightly sweet tuber with a taste and texture that are a cross between apple and celery. Grate it for salads, or slice it and eat it raw for a cool treat. It keeps its crisp texture when cubed and simmered for use in stews and soups.

KOMBU — a mineral-rich seaweed with broad flat fronds. Drop a small (3-6") strip into a pot of beans while cooking and it will enhance the flavour and make the beans more digestible. Discard when the beans are done.

LEMON GRASS — a tropical grass with a distinct lemon flavour that is used in Indonesian and Thai cooking and is a common ingredient in herbal teas. Heat dried lemon grass in oil, then remove and discard the lemon grass and use the flavoured oil for stir frying.

MACROBIOTICS — developed in Japan by Georges Ohsawa, macrobiotics is both a philosophy of living and a set of dietary principles. A macrobiotic diet consists of local, seasonal food, simply prepared. Macrobiotic principles encourage each individual to adapt their own diet with the end goal of achieving maximum health and harmony with the environment. Check the book section of your natural foods store for more information about macrobiotic philosophy and cooking.

MAPLE SYRUP — a golden sweet syrup that is processed from the sap of maple trees. This rich, delicious sweetener can seem like a luxury item, but the high cost begins to make more sense when you realize that it takes 40 gallons of sap (about the yield of one good-sized tree in a good year...) boiled down to make one gallon of maple syrup. Maple syrup comes in grades; grade A is more refined and lighter in colour while grade C is darker and richer in minerals. Maple syrup is sweet and potent, so you can use relatively small amounts and still have that distinctive and luxurious taste.

MIRIN — Japanese rice wine for cooking that is clear, sweet and potent. Use it sparingly to add a touch of sweetness to soups and sauces or to counteract the impact of other sour and salty tastes in cooking.

MISO — a salty Japanese paste that is low in fat, high in protein and B12, and full of flavour. It is made by cooking, aging and fermenting soybeans which are then sometimes mixed with other grains to make different flavours of miso such as genmai (brown rice), mugi (barley), or lighter, sweeter shiro (white rice). Misos vary in flavour and in colour from white to red to dark brown with many shades in between. Generally, misos can be used interchangeably, however the darker-coloured misos have been fermented longer and thus are stronger and saltier in flavour, so choose accordingly. Miso can be stored indefinitely at room temperature. It makes an excellent soup base when dissolved in hot water, but should not be boiled, as this destroys its nutritional properties.

NUTRITIONAL YEAST — not to be confused with baking yeast or brewer's yeast. It is not a leavening agent, but a condiment that is added to casseroles, salads, toast, popcorn and drinks, for its nutritional value and a flavour like cheese. Nutritional yeast, a pure yeast culture which is grown, fermented, pasteurized and dried, is high in B vitamins and protein. Similar to Engevita yeast and sometimes called good-tasting yeast, it can be stored indefinitely in an airtight container.

OILS — there has been an overwhelming flood of information on fats in our diet and on the desirability or importance of saturated or unsaturated fats. While trying to limit the intake of fats overall, one can still choose from a large variety of no-cholesterol vegetable oils, each with a slightly different flavour and with different nutritional properties. Use lighter oils such as sunflower or soy for baking and in dressings, and experiment with different varieties such as olive, walnut or sesame for their distinct flavour in cooking. Look for less refined, cold-pressed brands packaged in glass containers, and store them in the refrigerator to prevent them from going rancid.

PEPPERS — see the listing under "Chilis."

PESTO — an Italian sauce traditionally made by grinding fresh basil leaves with pine nuts, Parmesan cheese and olive oil to make a paste. This rich, fragrant sauce is then used on pasta or spread on bread. When fresh basil is plentiful, make up extra pesto and freeze it in airtight plastic containers. Or substitute fresh tarragon or parsley for the basil, or walnuts or pecans for the pine nuts for variations on a wonderful theme. Do *not* try to use dried herbs in place of fresh for making pesto — it does not work. There are several good packaged brands available or make your own vegan version from the pizza recipe on page 83.

PICANTE SAUCE — Picante is Spanish for hot or highly-seasoned. Picante sauce is a spicy and flavourful tomato-based sauce with diced vegetables, garlic, chilis and other seasonings. It is practically a way of life in the Southwest and Mexico, where it is used as a topping for chips, tacos, nachos, steamed vegetables and scrambled eggs. There are several good brands available commercially in mild, medium or hot strengths. Don't be tempted to omit this ingredient — find a brand that you like or make your own and use it liberally. Picante sauce is sometimes called salsa, a name that is loaned to a Mexican dance that also puts fire in your veins.

PINE NUTS — also called pignolas or piñons, pine nuts are harvested from pine cones, and are used in both Mediterranean and Southwestern U.S. cooking. An oily, yellowish kernel with a slight taste of resin, they can be eaten raw or toasted, ground or whole. They are an indispensible ingredient in pesto. For toasting instructions, see page 93.

POLENTA — a porridge of boiled cornmeal used in Italian cooking or eaten as a side dish. See Eggplant Parmesan recipe, page 63.

RICE SYRUP — a sweetener with a delicate taste, rice syrup is a complex carbohydrate derived by malting cooked brown rice. It is less sweet than honey, but can be used as a substitute for honey or sugar in baking and sauces.

SHIITAKE MUSHROOMS — available fresh or dried, these large Japanese mushrooms have a chewy texture and a distinctive flavour. To re-hydrate dried shiitakes, boil for 5 minutes, then set aside to soak for 15 to 20 minutes. Remove and discard the tough stems, and use the soaking liquid in soup broth.

SHOYU — a Japanese soy sauce. See 'Tamari" listing page 129.

SOBA — Japanese noodles made from buckwheat flour, either entirely or mixed with wheat flour. When made of 100% buckwheat, they make a delicious and useful alternative for those allergic to wheat, though pure buckwheat noodles are a little heavier in texture. Cook using the 'shocking' method, see entry on page 18. Used in soups or noodle dishes, soba noodles are excellent served hot or chilled.

SOYBEANS — the soybean, used extensively in the Orient, is a highly nutritious bean, containing more protein than any other bean in a proportion of essential amino acids that is closer to that of animal products. Indeed, it is such a good and widely used source of protein that is is referred to as the "boneless meat," or the "vegetable cow" of the Orient. Its bland flavour is turned to an advantage as it is added to dishes and drinks to boost their nutritional content; it takes on the flavour of whatever sauce, spice or marinade is used. In the Orient, soybeans traditionally have been ground into flour or made into a dairy substitute called soymilk, or aged or fermented to create tofu, tempeh, tamari, miso and other soyfoods — see these individual entries for more information. Soybeans require a longer cooking time than most beans — letting them simmer for 4 to 5 hours after soaking will render them more digestible. See the section on Dried Beans, page 133.

In the case of the fermented soyfoods like tempeh and miso, a mold culture is added to the soybeans, developing microorganisms that alter the composition of the food, giving a stronger and more pronounced taste to it. Fermented foods like tempeh or wine, cheese, sauerkraut, sourdough bread, beer and pickles in the West, improve the intestinal flora, aiding in the digestion of dense protein and carbohydrate foods. They are more nutritious and digestible than the unprocessed original food, and help the digestibility of foods eaten along with it. In the case of high-protein soybeans which are more difficult to digest in their whole form, the natural processing adds to the assimilation of their considerable nutrients.

Roasted soybeans, sometimes called soy nuts, have been commercially roasted to make a crunchy snack food.

SOYMILK — a non-dairy beverage for drinking or cooking derived from cooked soybeans, sometimes with sweeteners or flavourings added. Because soymilk is cholesterol-free and contains no lactose, it is a good choice for people who are allergic to dairy products. Soymilk is now available plain or flavoured with vanilla or carob, and there are many brands which can be stored unopened in the pantry, needing refrigeration only after opening. Use plain soymilk as the base for creamy soups, in sauces or dressings, and use the flavoured kinds for baking or drinking.

STOCK — vegetable broth or stock is easily made from vegetable ends and peels. Bring 8 or more cups of spring water to a boil in a pot. Rinse and add the ends or stems of celery, parsley, green beans, green onions, spinach, lettuce or zucchini for a green stock. For a stock that is richer in flavour and brown in colour, add carrot peels and the skins and ends of onions and garlic. Toss in a bay leaf, cracked peppercorns and herbs. Avoid using cabbage, broccoli, cauliflower or peppers, as they will give the stock a strong or bitter flavour.

Boil the water and vegetables until the water is reduced by half. Discard the vegetables and strain the broth through a fine sieve. Use the broth as a base for soups or add to sauces. Stock will keep for 3 to 4 days in the refrigerator in an airtight container. Or freeze the stock in ice cube trays, then store the frozen broth cubes in a plastic bag in the freezer, thawing and using as needed.

SUCANAT — a substitute for brown sugar, Sucanat is a natural sweetener that is granulated from dried cane juice. It is less refined than white granulated sugar. Substitute for equal amounts of white or brown sugar.

SWEETENERS — there are a variety of sweeteners available at natural foods markets; honey, maple syrup, rice malt, Sucanat, etc. See these individual entries for more information. Having a "sweet tooth" is a hard habit to break, but try experimenting with alternative sweeteners that are less refined than white sugar.

TAHINI — sesame butter, a spreadable paste made from sesame seeds, similar to but thinner in consistency than peanut butter. Rich in both calcium and flavour, it can be used alone as a sandwich spread, blended in to thicken sauces and gravies, or mixed with beans to make spreads and dips such as hummus. Store in refrigerator for best results.

TAMARI — Japanese soy sauce, but usually made without wheat or the additives and colouring agents found in many commercial soy sauces. An indispensible flavouring, it adds a rich salty taste and dark brown colour when cooking soups, sauces, marinades or vegetables, and can be used as a lower-sodium replacement for salt at the table. Shoyu is similar to tamari, but may contain wheat. Check the label, as the two names are sometimes used interchangeably here in the West. Please do not be tempted to use the commercial brands that have long been available here, as the sweeteners and other additives make for a far inferior taste.

TEMPEH — a soyfood native to Indonesia where householders often made tempeh on a daily basis, as yogurt or bread is in other cultures. Tempeh contains all the nutrients of soybeans as it uses the bean in its whole form. It has a satisfying chewy texture and a flavour that can be compared to nuts, mushrooms or bacon. It is wonderful marinated, sautéed or baked as a meat substitute in loafs, patés and casseroles. Our favourite way to prepare it is to cube it, marinate it in tamari and assorted spices, then toast it on an oiled cookie sheet at 400 degrees F for 10 to 15 minutes until it is crispy. Use these toasted cubes in bean dishes, stir frys, or as "croutons" for salads.

Tempeh is sold in the freezer section in 6" x 6" squares which are about ½-inch thick. To thaw, leave in the refrigerator overnight, at room temperature for 2 to 3 hours or steam over boiling water for 20 to 30 minutes before preparing as directed.

TOASTED SESAME OIL — processed from toasted sesame seeds, this oil is darker in colour than plain sesame oil, with a distinctive aroma. It is to be used more as a flavouring agent than a cooking oil. Used sparingly, it lends a potent and wonderful taste to dressings and stir frys.

TOFU — another traditional soyfood, tofu is made by a process very similar to cheese making, using the "milk" from cooked and ground soybeans. The end product is a smooth, bland, slightly spongy block or cake that is high in protein and low in fat. It can be used raw or sautéed or baked to add to stir frys, casseroles, salads, sandwiches, desserts and more. Tofu is usually found packaged or sold in bulk in half-pound blocks or cubes in the cooler section of your local store — it has become so much more widely known here in the West in the last few years that it can now be found in most regular grocery stores.

Store tofu in the refrigerator for 3 days to a week. It shoud be stored in water, and the water should be drained and replaced every day or so to keep the tofu fresh.

Tofu can also be frozen — it will keep for 6 weeks in the freezer. Freezing changes the texture of tofu to a more spongy consistency. This works well for dishes when a chewier texture is desired. Thaw by soaking the frozen tofu in boiling water, then press, drain and use as desired.

Tofu soaks up moisture; this means it absorbs sauces and marinades well. But since it is stored in water, it should be pressed and drained before use to reduce the water content; this gives it a firmer texture and allows better absorption of whatever sauce or dressing is being used. To press the tofu, simply place it on a plate or tray with a rim, place another plate on top of the cube of tofu, and then place a weight — such as a heavy tin can — on top. Be sure the weight is evenly distributed, and heavy enough to press but not flatten the tofu cube. Leave it for 15 to 30 minutes, then remove the weights, drain the expressed water and prep the tofu as usual. We have two favourite ways of eating tofu. The simplest is to mash raw, drained tofu and combine it with mayonnaise and the herbs of your choice to make a spread, like the devilled tofu on page 115. (Alternately, mash it with a couple of tablespoons of tamari and nutritional yeast, adding diced green onions for a delicious variation.) Or, press and drain the tofu, cut it into cubes or thin strips, marinate it in a little tamari with grated fresh ginger and bake on an oiled cookie sheet for 10 to 15 minutes until it is crunchy. Add to stir frys or noodle dishes, but be sure to make extra as these crispy tofu treats are easy to nibble on while you are cooking.

UDON NOODLES — thin, flat Japanese noodles made from whole wheat flour. Cook using the "shocking" method described on page 18. The texture of udon noodles is particularly good for chilled noodle dishes in the summer.

UMEBOSHI PLUM PASTE — a rosy paste made of Japanese plums that are pickled in salt with beefsteak leaves. Intensely sour and salty, small amounts can be stirred into soups and dressings to enhance flavour. It is also believed to have medicinal properties helpful in relieving acid indigestion and some headaches.

VEGAN — a vegan diet does not include the use of any product derived from animals. Vegan vegetarians avoid eating flesh and using by-products such as milk or honey. There are books available at your natural foods store with more information on vegan principles.

A GUIDE TO GRAINS AND BEANS

Whole grains have been the basis of human diet for thousands of years, replaced to a greater extent by meat and dairy products in industrialized nations during the last few hundred years.

A return to a "meal" (literally ground grain) centred on grains is a healthy, ecological and tasty choice. Unrefined grains, more nutritious and flavourful than refined, are generally used in The Big Carrot recipes.

RICE: Staple of more than half the world's population, rice is versatile and poses no problems for most allergy sufferers. We use brown rice instead of white; it takes about three times as long to cook, but it is less refined and thus offers more fibre and food value.

Long Grain: is best suited to salads and pilafs as the grains stay separate and "fluffy" in cooking.

Short Grain: higher in protein than long grain, has a stickier texture when cooked. It is a good all-purpose rice ideal for casseroles and puddings.

WILD RICE: Not a rice at all, but the seed of a wild grass traditionally harvested by native people in northern Canada.

Its robust flavour is excellent combined with brown rice in stuffing, pilafs and salads.

BARLEY: Unpearled barley (without the husk, bran and germ removed) is available in natural food stores. It is light brown in colour and is often used for soups and stews as it thickens the broth. Whole kernel barley can also be used in salads as a change from rice.

MILLET: This grain, relegated to the lowly ranks of birdseed in Canada, is eaten by millions daily in Asia and Africa. Millet is a more nearly complete protein than any other grain and is particularly easy to digest. This small, seed-like grain has a mild flavour and is suitable for gluten-free and allergy-restricted diets. Cooked whole, in casseroles, patties, puddings or ground into flour for breads, pancakes, muffins and other baked goods, it is one of the most versatile grains.

BULGUR: This Middle Eastern staple is wheat that has been steamed and dried, then cracked into small pieces. Often used in salads or in pilaf style dishes.

CORNMEAL: Aside from corn on the cob and popcorn, we hardly know North America's original grain at all! Field corn, different from the sweet corn eaten fresh, is dried and ground into meal and flour. Traditionally used in combination with beans, it can take the shape of tortillas, Johnny cakes (from "journey cakes" used in travel), bread, porridge or casseroles.

QUINOA: Sacred grain of the ancient Aztecs, quinoa has grown in popularity in North America where it is now cultivated. It contains a proportion of amino acids close to the ideal, a nutty flavour and light texture that is appealing. Used alone or in combination with other grains in salads, it can also substitute for other grains in entrées when a light texture is desired.

WHOLE GRAIN COOKING AND PROPORTIONS

(for 1 cup dry measure of grain)

Grain	Water	Cooking Time	Yield
Brown Rice	2 cups	45 minutes	3 cups
Bulgur	2 cups	15 minutes	2½ cups
Millet	3 cups	40 minutes	3½ cups
Wild rice	3 cups	45-60 minutes	4 cups
Barley	3 cups	50-60 minutes	3½ cups
Cornmeal	4-6 cups	50-60 minutes	5-6 cups
Quinoa	2 cups	15 minutes	3 cups

COOKING INSTRUCTIONS: Bring suggested quantity of spring water to a boil in a heavy-bottomed pot with a lid. Add grain and ½ teaspoon salt if desired, stir and reduce heat to a simmer. Cook, covered, over low heat for the amount of time recommended in the above chart.

DRIED BEANS & PEAS

Beans and peas, sometimes called pulses, are an important source of protein and iron and supply sizeable amounts of copper, B vitamins and complex carbohydrates. They are a staple food in countries where little meat is eaten.

COOKING METHODS:

Three methods can be used for cooking beans. Each uses three cups water for every cup of dried beans unless otherwise specified in a recipe. One cup of dried beans or peas will yield approximately 2½ cups cooked. Before soaking and cooking, all beans and peas need to be sorted through to check for small stones and clumps of mud which should be discarded. They should then be rinsed in a colander to remove dust and soaked. Pre-soaking will make the beans cook more evenly and quickly.

1) Slow Soaking and Cooking: Place beans in a large pot, add three cups of water for every cup of dried beans and soak, covered, for 6 to 8 hours or overnight in the refrigerator or on the countertop (do not leave on stovetop). Add more water if needed to be sure beans remain covered with liquid, then proceed to cook as recipe directs.

2) Quick Soaking and Cooking: Place beans in a large pot, add three cups of water for every cup of dried beans, and bring to a boil. Remove from heat and let stand for 1 hour, then proceed to cook as recipe suggests.

3) Cooking: If beans are not pre-soaked, add 3 cups of water for every cup of dried beans and bring beans to a boil. Reduce heat to a simmer and cook, stirring occasionally until tender and adding water as needed to keep beans covered with liquid, and cook over low heat to prevent scorching. Beans that are not pre-soaked will take longer to cook.

Do not salt beans until end of cooking as it makes the beans tough and harder to cook. Slow and gentle cooking of beans brings out their flavour. Remove and discard any foam that forms on beans while cooking. Keep cooked beans refrigerated and bring to a boil before re-using.

SPECIAL COOKING NEEDS

Cooking times vary from bean to bean and with different dishes. For bean salads, beans should be cooked slightly less so that they will retain their shape and not break down. For soups, casseroles and especially for making spreads like hummus or refried beans, they should be cooked until very tender.

Garbanzos (chick peas) and **soybeans** require a longer cooking time than other beans, 4 to 5 hours to be properly cooked and easier to eat. They can be frozen between soaking and cooking to shorten the cooking time and increase palatability and ease of digestion. For chick peas, drain and freeze. Soybeans should be frozen with some of their soaking water.

Peas, including split green and yellow, **blackeye peas, mung beans, aduki beans** and **lentils** of many types do not require soaking. Their cooking time ranges from ¾ hour to 1½ hours. They break down easily and are therefore excellent in soups, stews and patés.

FLAVOUR AND DIGESTIBILITY

To retain flavour and nutrients, cook beans in their soaking water.
If you have trouble digesting beans, throw away soaking water or feed the water to your plants, and use fresh water to cook. In all methods, a piece of kelp (kombu) sea vegetable can be added during cooking to help the digestibility of the beans. Eating small amounts to start and chewing well also helps.

THE BIG CARROT AT WORK
AS A WORKER COOPERATIVE

In the business of selling and promoting healthy food, The Big Carrot is further distinguished by its structure as a worker cooperative. After a working for a probationary period, employees make a long-term commitment to the store, invest money, become co-owners, and make decisions as a group about how the store is run.

All of the staff at The Big Carrot share in the operation of the store. We have a stake in its success and a commitment to the quality of the products that we sell. The goals of The Big Carrot are summed up in our mission statement, as follows:

We share a vision that combines a commitment to natural foods with the process of building a democratic workplace. The Big Carrot is a place where people are able to choose realistic alternatives in terms of what they eat and the way food is grown and processed. As worker-owners, we seek to keep personal control and choice over the quality of the food we sell and the nature of our work environment.

Our purpose is to provide our customers with the finest quality and selection of natural foods, backed by friendly service and information about our products and goals. We actively encourage increased production and distribution of organic and additive-free products, and actively support sustainable agriculture and ecologically sound practices. We seek to offer satisfying, gainful employment in a fair and productive workplace.

We have a commitment to offering the finest quality in wholesome and organic foods. The Big Carrot seeks to offer complete one-stop shopping for natural foods customers, with high-quality products, friendly service, competitive prices and wide selection. Our goal is to continue as innovative leaders within the industry.

Our purchasing policies are designed to support the ongoing development of a local network of natural foods suppliers. The Big Carrot purchases from small local and organic producers whenever possible. Furthermore, each product has to meet a set of standards designed to guide departmental buying.

Our pricing policy is to be competitive with other natural food stores. Many of our products are new and are initially supplied to us at a premium, but through our work with local producers, we hope to make organic foods more affordable over time.

We believe public education in social and environmental issues is a key to the health and prosperity of individuals and the community as a whole. One of our goals is to develop a skilled and knowledgeable staff able to introduce customers to these issues and to alternative high-quality products.

Our success is measured in customer and worker satisfaction, and by our work in the development of a sustainable and healthy food system. Financial success means paying our workers wages and benefits comparable with industry averages, while maintaining competitive prices and providing added incentives for our members. We direct a share of our profits, as well as contributing volunteer time and money throughout the year, to other co-ops and to social change, agricultural and humanitarian groups.

Acting on the belief that change can come through collective action, The Big Carrot is intentionally organized as a worker cooperative. The cooperative structure represents a way in which a small group of people can create a meaningful business.

The Big Carrot's members are committed to maintaining and refining the cooperative structure in order to utilize the strengths of a growing membership base. Within this framework, each worker is eligible to be a member and every member has one vote in our general meetings. In making a financial investment, each member accepts a personal responsibility for the success of our co-op.

Since the store was started in 1983, the following people have been member-owners of The Big Carrot:

Bob Allen, Fernando Amaya, Miquel Amaya, Heather Barclay, Aziza Bellair, Les Bowser, Maxine Cassidy, Martin Cerrone, David Dennis, Paul Gibbard, Ellen Godfrey, Meri Hanlin, Kar-in Hansen, John Hopperton, Akemi Kobayashi, Daiva Kryzanauskas, Brad LaMarsh, Jane Langmuir, Jerry Lewycky, Grant MacKinnon, Mary Lou Morgan, Kate Middleton, Lisa Perrotta, Amelia Quilty-Peters, Luanne Rayvals, Pat Smith, Lockwood Spafford, Judith Stamp, Kent Wakely

The Cooks of The Big Carrot Kitchen, Spring 1989 (left to right):
John Ghitan, Nelly Hotke, Anne Lukin,
Gladys Amaya, Sharon Bishop, Paula Ring

INDEX